To Joe Zukin,

With my best wishes,

Ed Lindop

March, 1979

White House Sportsmen

Edmund Lindop and Joseph Jares

Illustrated with photographs

HOUGHTON MIFFLIN COMPANY BOSTON

The Riverside Press Cambridge/1964

CONTENTS

On the Gridiron

I GREATLY admire football," President Theodore Roosevelt wrote to his son Ted in 1903. Although he never played the game himself, the robust Chief Executive was convinced that "to develop the simple but all-essential traits which go to make up manliness . . . there is no better sport than football."

Roosevelt was eager to have his own sons play this vigorous game. He once said that "if any one of them would weigh a possible broken bone against the glory of being chosen to play on Harvard's football team I would disinherit him." Two of his sons, Ted and Kermit, played football at Groton, the fashionable preparatory school, while their father was President.

From the White House the former Rough Rider frequently corresponded with the boys about their enthusiastic but unspectacular gridiron efforts. "Who plays opposite you at end?" he asked of Kermit. "Do you find you can get down well under the ball to tackle the fullback? How are you tackling?"

In his own strenuous life the rougher the going, the better Roosevelt liked it. So the rugged nature of football appealed to this White House sportsman. He admitted that "the very things that make it a good game make it a rough game." Every man on the team, he felt, should play with all his might from the time he ran out on the field until the final whistle blew. This same driving determination was also Roosevelt's formula for achieving success in other fields. His famous advice to the young people of America was phrased in football terms: "Don't flinch, don't foul, hit the line hard!"

But during Roosevelt's administration the sport of football was in serious trouble because many players resorted to brutality and foul tactics. Football was then in its infancy, and there were few rules to govern the game. The ball was advanced by mass plays in which all the players on the offensive team threw themselves in steamroller fashion against the defenders. Brute force alone determined whether the ball would be pushed ahead. Slugging, kicking, and gouging were common practices in this era when the referees had little power to keep the game fair and clean.

In the first five years of this century forty-five players were killed and several hundred were seriously injured in college games. During the 1905 season a player in a Pennsylvania college died from a kick in the head, a Harvard student had his skull cracked, a tackle from Columbia had his vision so badly impaired he had to drop out of school, and a wild fistfight erupted between Wesleyan and Columbia players that had to be broken up by the police. The Chicago *Tribune* reported the horrifying statistics of football casualties for the bloody

1905 season in college and high school games: eighteen deaths and 159 serious injuries.

A clamor arose throughout the country that such brutality must be stopped. Frightened parents forbade their young sons to play the dangerous game. Newspaper editorials suggested that soccer might be substituted for football as a safer, cleaner sport. Officials at Columbia University announced that their school was abandoning the game of football, and President Eliot of Harvard was anxious to follow suit. Football was in danger of disappearing from the American scene, and many school authorities felt that the end of the game could not come too soon.

President Roosevelt, hearing the complaints against football, was greatly distressed that the game had gotten out of hand. "Very emphatically," he angrily declared, "we do not approve of brutality of any kind." But while he condemned the unfair tactics that were ruining football, he refused to agree with the critics who wanted to abolish the game. He maintained that football, if properly played and carefully supervised, could build character rather than break bodies. Instead of eliminating the sport, students and faculties "should insist upon the umpires putting a peremptory stop to any kind of slugging or kindred brutality in the game."

The President decided to put his views about football before the public. In 1905 he invited to a Washington conference the athletic officials from some of the leading Eastern colleges where football was played. The President pulled no punches with the assembled delegates. He told them he had called this meeting in the "public interest," and he warned them "to make the game of football a rather less homicidal pastime" if they wanted the sport to survive.

The faculty men talked frankly about the vicious practices that were spoiling the game. Before leaving Washington they promised the President they would try to prevent their players from using such tactics in future games. But the chief accomplishment of this White House conference was that for the first time nationwide attention had been focused on the need to reform rather than destroy football. The following year representatives from twenty-eight colleges met to adopt new rules, and in 1910 another intercollegiate rules committee made major changes which led to a much safer and more scientific brand of football.

While Theodore Roosevelt helped save football, another President, as a young man, coached the sport. When Woodrow Wilson enrolled at Princeton University in 1875, he was intrigued by the new exciting game. He did not have the physique and skill to be a good player, but he attended practices regularly and studied every team maneuver. In those days there were no professional football coaches, and the Princeton team was coached by a committee composed of students from the three upper classes. Wilson showed such an avid interest in the technical end of the game that his classmates elected him to the coaching committee.

Many problems confronted the student coaches in that early period before rules and regulations had been commonly agreed upon. Even the number of players on a team varied from school to school; for example, Princeton had to put fifteen men on the field against Harvard and only eleven against Yale. Moreover, when Wilson started coaching, the old English scrummage was still being used for putting the ball in play. The ball was placed on the ground between the two teams, and players from both sides tried to work it between their feet (they were prohibited from using their hands) until it was kicked out of scrummage. Wilson and other early coaches argued against this system. The game would be improved, they felt, if one team were given possession of the ball and allowed to snap it back to start a play in an orderly manner. This would make it possible to have prearranged plays and special assignments for each man. Football could then become a sport of skill as well as a battle of brawn.

The coaches who favored a new offensive system for football eventually won the argument. By the time that Wilson had become a professor of history and political economy at Wesleyan University in 1888, the American scrimmage had replaced the English scrummage on gridirons throughout the nation. The youthful professor, eager to devise new plays that could be adapted to the scrimmage system, volunteered to work with the football team. Every afternoon following classes Professor Wilson strolled out to the football field and helped his young charges prepare for their games. Together with two other associate coaches, he introduced at Wesleyan many new pigskin features. These included quick line plunges, the "crisscross" or double pass, and the practice of giving protection to ball carriers on end runs.

Wesleyan rooters claimed Professor Wilson was the inventor of a series of "rotation plays." These were various sequences of plays that followed one another without signals. In the 1889 game against Pennsylvania, a traditional rival, the Wesleyan team waited until it had advanced the ball to within a short distance of the Pennsylvania goal line. Then the quarterback suddenly clapped his hands, and the "rotation" went into effect. In rapid succession, without pausing for signals, the Wesleyan men executed a series of carefully rehearsed plays. The Pennsylvania defenders were stunned by the swiftness of the attack and confused by the lack of signals. Wesleyan marched to a quick touchdown that spelled defeat for Pennsylvania, and much of the credit for the victory was attributed to Professor Wilson's clever strategy.

Besides helping his players outwit the opposition, Wilson generated an enthusiasm that inspired the men of Wesleyan in their battles on the gridiron. In the past, whenever Wesleyan players had faced the superb teams from Yale, they had been resigned to defeat even before they took the field. Their only desire was to play well enough to hold down the score. But when Wilson arrived on the scene, he would have no part of this defeatist attitude. "Go in and win," the young professor told the players before the game started. "You can lick Yale as well as any other team. Go after their scalps. Don't admit for a moment that they can beat you." After Wilson's fighting remarks, the Wesleyan men charged onto the field, eager to do battle for their alma mater. Although they were no match for the very strong Yale team, Wilson's players earned respect as they went down fighting all the way.

On at least one occasion Wilson's spirited support for the Wesleyan team spread to the rooters too. This was on a rainy Thanksgiving Day in 1889 when Lehigh was leading the Red and Black team by two touchdowns. A cloud of gloom hung over the silent Wesleyan fans who sensed that their team was headed for certain defeat. Suddenly a man clad in heavy boots and a black rubber overcoat left the sideline and walked in front of the rickety bleachers. In a defiant voice that bristled through the rain, Professor Wilson scolded the listless Wesleyan rooters for not supporting their team with cheers and yells. Thundering the cry that all was not yet lost, he stirred new hope in the dejected student body.

Excitement filled the air as Wilson began to lead the aroused spectators in the Wesleyan yell, beating time for them with his closed umbrella. Soon the yell swelled into a deafening roar, which the players could not help but hear. This may have been the spark that ignited the team to fight back. For the Wesleyan players suddenly seemed to gain new confidence, and they pushed over two touchdowns that tied the score. After the final whistle had blown, some of the Lehigh players asked who was the inspired Wesleyan cheer leader. Much to their surprise they learned that the rousing noisemaker was a soft-spoken history professor.

In the autumn of 1890 Wilson became a professor of jurisprudence at his own alma mater, Princeton. Those were dark days for the once-powerful Princeton Tigers; graduation had left only three members of the championship team of 1889. The practice of hiring regular coaches had not yet begun, so it was a welcome sight one afternoon in October when the lanky new professor came out to the football field. Wilson modestly volunteered to help coach the inexperienced team, and his offer was quickly accepted. Patiently he set out to correct the players' mistakes, teach them new plays, and inspire them with his contagious enthusiasm for the sport. Rain or shine, during the entire season he turned out daily for practices.

Swinging a cane and wearing a collegian's cap, a loose-fitting jacket, rolled-up trousers, and red leather shoes, the future President of the United States intently followed every play of the Princeton eleven. Occasionally he would call the men to the sideline to explain some new strategy that he had planned. The task of perfecting the game provided difficult problems even for a brilliant thinker like Wilson. One of the problems which Wilson never could solve was how to stop a cer-

tain Yale guard from opening huge holes in the Princeton line. But none of the other teams could stop this
guard either, and the incomparable "Pudge" Heffelfinger
became one of the game's immortal players.

At the conclusion of the 1890 season Woodrow Wilson's coaching days came to an end when he was appointed Chairman of the Committee on Outdoor Sports.
In this highly important faculty post Wilson worked to
improve the athletic program at Princeton. He reor-
ganized the whole system of athletic management and
launched a campaign that brought his school better
athletic fields, training facilities, and sports equipment.
Wilson carried out these duties so effectively that he
continued to head the Princeton athletic program until
he was appointed president of the university.

At the opposite end of the country from Princeton, in
California, another future President labored to bring
football to his school. One of the first students to enroll
when Stanford University opened its doors in 1891 was
a chunky youngster named Herbert Hoover. He and
some of the other students who were interested in sports
decided to organize a football team at their new school.
They chalked out a rough gridiron on a lumpy hay field
and began to practice. Only a few of the youths had
played on any team before, but whatever they lacked in
experience was made up for in enthusiasm. This cocky
lot of green players had enough courage to challenge the
neighboring University of California to a game.

California had a strong eleven which had gained experience by swamping local high school and club teams. The boys from Berkeley regarded lightly the challenge from upstart Stanford, and they relished the chance to add the new college team to their impressive list of beaten foes. But the Stanford Indians were determined to scalp the haughty Golden Bears, and they worked out feverishly for the big game. Hoover could not play well enough to make the squad. His classmates, however, knew he had a good mind for business and asked him to be the team manager.

To Hoover fell the important task of arranging all the details for the Far West's first intercollegiate football game. He rented the Haight Street baseball park in San Francisco for $250. Then he approached a sports dealer with an order for the players' uniforms. Since the team had no funds, the uniforms had to be purchased on credit. The youthful manager kept his fingers crossed and prayed that enough spectators would attend the game to keep him from going into debt.

On the day of the big game Hoover's worries about gate receipts vanished when he saw the long lines of fans arriving in buggies and carriages. So many people poured into the park that the sellers ran out of tickets, and gold and silver coins began spilling over the bags in the ticket booths. Hoover frantically dispatched his assistants to comb the neighborhood for dishpans, buckets, or any kind of containers that could hold the overflowing coins. Then he quickly assembled a corps of college boys to escort past the gate those fans who had paid for admission but had no tickets.

Meanwhile, the players raced out on the field only to discover that they had no football. The young Stanford manager was horrified when he realized he had overlooked this one small detail! Hastily he sent downtown for a football. The messenger finally located one, but it had no bladder. So he quickly substituted a punching bag bladder and raced back to the field with a rather odd-shaped but precious ball.

The game had been delayed half an hour. But this did not dampen the spirit of the inspired Stanford team that proceeded to outplay the heavily favored California squad. "To our astonishment we won," Hoover proudly remarked years later in recalling the memorable event that occurred on March 19, 1892. Stanford's surprising 14–10 victory marked the beginning of a great traditional rivalry known as The Big Game, and some fans claimed that the first of these games was the biggest one of all.

Unfortunately, the conscientious Stanford team manager was too busy to see the great game he had arranged. His duties also prevented him from taking part in the jubilant victory celebrations. "After the game," Hoover explained, "the California manager and I returned to a hotel with our money, now transferred to grain bags, and sat up most of the night counting it. I had never seen $30,000 before." Probably the young undergraduate was somewhat nervous about guarding so much money until the bank opened the next day, but in his memoirs he made only one observation: "We were well financed for the next season."

Two Presidents who as youths diligently worked to become good football players were Franklin D. Roosevelt and John F. Kennedy. Neither of them, however, had the physique to match his ambition. At Groton, young Roosevelt went out for football, but the best he could do was land a spot on a fourth-string eleven. As Dr. Endicott Peabody, Groton's headmaster, explained, "Athletically he was rather too slight for success." Later, when he went to Harvard, F.D.R. was very eager to make good in football. However, weighing only 146 pounds, he was much too light to be a sturdy tackle or guard, and he was not sufficiently agile for the backfield. So he tried out for end on the freshman team but lasted only two weeks. As a small consolation he did manage to become captain of one of the scrub teams, but this was a far cry from the gridiron role he dreamed of playing.

Kennedy first played football in grade school at Dexter, a private academy. As a teenager at Choate School he went out for the sport but failed to make the varsity. Like F.D.R., Kennedy tried out for end on the Harvard freshman team. Through sheer persistence and hard work he made the squad. "Jack would not be considered a top-notch player because he lacked weight and swiftness," recalled Congressman Torbert Macdonald, his college roommate and a former Harvard football star. "However, he practiced diligently and made the most of his natural talents. And he was very determined." As a sophomore Kennedy was dropped to the junior varsity, but he continued to play with fearless abandon. Scrimmaging one afternoon against the much heavier varsity team, Jack received the serious spinal injury that was to follow him into adulthood.

Although his injury forced him to give up football in college, Kennedy never lost his passion for playing the game. While serving in Congress he occasionally would leave his office early, change into an old sweatshirt and sneakers, and hurry over to a Georgetown playground to toss passes and run plays with a gang of high school boys. Few of the teenagers knew they were playing with a congressman. Probably none of them suspected that their tall, lanky teammate, who wiped the sweat from his forehead with the sleeve of his faded sweatshirt, would someday be elected President of the United States.

Touch football was the favorite outdoor game of the large Kennedy family, including the wives and in-laws. The spirited games on the lawn at their Hyannis Port estate became a famous trademark of the clan. After choosing up sides, the two Kennedy teams would battle each other with relentless fury. Wives would straight-arm their husbands, sisters would shove their in-laws, brothers would lunge viciously at one another. Everyone played with a desperate determination to win, and nothing short of an all-out effort was enough. It was considered a great compliment when the President once said of his sister-in-law: "Ethel's really good. You ought to see her run and pass."

Injuries and accidents had to be expected now and then from such a rough sport. Robert Kennedy, the President's brother, once was so anxious to score a touchdown that he ran headlong into a barbed wire fence and covered his face with blood. On the day before his own marriage the President fell into a rosebush while trying to snag a pass, and he appeared at his wedding with scratches adorning his face. A short time later his new bride became a football casualty. Jacqueline Kennedy broke her ankle in one of the family games and retired permanently to the sidelines, leaving the sport to the sturdier members of the clan.

Although Kennedy was the only Chief Executive who continued to play football in his mature years, the White House occupant who had the greatest talent for the game was Dwight Eisenhower. But as a high school student in Abilene, Kansas, Ike had to hurdle many obstacles before he could even play on a regular team. In those days sports at Abilene High were not included in the regular school activities. The school hired no coaches and furnished no money for athletic equipment, uniforms, or transportation to games. But the students decided they wanted to have their own football team, so they formed an Abilene High School Association to try to raise the necessary funds. Eisenhower was elected president of the new group.

The association members rolled up their sleeves and began collecting donations from the local citizens. In time they managed to scrape together enough money to outfit a team, but there was nothing left in the treasury after the uniforms and equipment were purchased. A crisis arose when Abilene had to play Chapman High, twelve miles away. "What will we do?" the boys asked Ike. "We don't have the money for train tickets."

Ike thought the problem over carefully, trying to arrive at some solution. Finally he hit upon an idea. "We'll hop a freight train," he exclaimed. "If we're all on the same train, we'll outnumber the brakemen. Even if they see us they won't dare try to shove us all off." So the following Saturday morning the entire Abilene team bummed a ride to Chapman, and after chalking up a hard-earned victory they joyfully rode the rails home.

Eisenhower was graduated in 1909, but he returned to high school the following fall for some more courses. There were no rules then against graduates playing on the football team, and Ike could not resist the opportunity to suit up for another season. His teammates eagerly welcomed him back, for Eisenhower had been Abilene's best tackle. He was powerful and fast enough to open gaping holes for the ball carriers, and his defensive play was outstanding.

Against Salina, one of Abilene's toughest foes, Ike played his most brilliant game. The Salina boys had a tricky delayed-buck play that had deceived all their earlier opponents and led to large gains. The play worked effectively the first couple of times it was run over Ike's position. But then Ike caught on to what was happening, and every time Salina tried this play again he swiftly sidestepped the interference and charged in to tackle the ball carrier. On offense Ike was also a stand-out, helping to pave the way for two Abilene drives that resulted in touchdowns.

Toward the end of the game the trailing Salina team became desperate, and some rough play occurred in which one of Ike's teammates was knocked unconscious. Thinking the injury had been deliberate, Ike fumed with rage. He began tackling and blocking with a savage fury that staggered and dazed several Salina players. Again and again he broke through the line to nail the Salina runners for big losses. After the game the coach of the defeated Salina eleven praised Eisenhower's rugged performance and said he wished he were on his team.

Ike was admitted to West Point in 1911, and he played the first year on the Cullum Hall squad, Army's freshman team. The following season he made the Army varsity as the second-string left halfback. Ike was assigned to understudy Geoffrey Keyes, the Cadets' great star of the previous year. But Keyes was injured in a practice session before the 1912 season began. So the name of the sophomore from Kansas appeared in the starting line-up for the kick-off against Stevens, Army's first opponent. The Cadets feared that the loss of Keyes would hurt their chances. His substitute, however, turned in such a sterling performance that before the game was over the West Pointers practically forgot that their star halfback was riding the bench. Ike tackled hard, blocked expertly, and carried the ball with tremendous drive. He did more than his share in helping Army run up a 27–0 score over Stevens.

The following week the Cadets faced Rutgers, and Eisenhower again replaced the ailing Keyes. Leading his team to a smashing 19–0 victory, Ike turned in another brilliant game. Eastern sports writers were now convinced that Army had a great prospect in this hard-driving sophomore back. Some writers dubbed him the "Kansas Cyclone," and others called him the "Huge Kansan." Even the cautious *New York Times* lauded the future President as "one of the most promising backs in Eastern football."

Army played Yale the next week, and Keyes, having recovered, returned to the starting line-up. Powerful Yale had one of the best teams in the East. The rugged eleven from Old Eli took a 6–0 lead, and then dug in to prevent Army from scoring. Ike watched most of the game from the bench, but the coach sent him in for the final few minutes. Powering his way through the tiring Yale line, the 190-pound Kansan carried the ball for several large gains. He drove his team near the Yale goal, and the excited West Point rooters cheered for a last-minute touchdown. But the timekeeper's gun sounded before Army could reach pay dirt.

Colgate was next on the schedule, and Ike helped the

Cadets march to an 18–7 win. One of the reporters was so impressed with the sophomore halfback that he wrote, "Eisenhower in the fourth period could not be stopped." The following week Army tangled with the mighty Carlisle Indians led by Jim Thorpe, one of the greatest all-around players ever to don a football uniform. The legendary Thorpe did everything splendidly — run, pass, kick, block, tackle. Every team tried frantically to "stop Thorpe," but the sensational Indian could not be halted.

Ike played his heart out that afternoon. On both offense and defense he put forth a tremendous effort. Once he and a teammate ganged up on the amazing Thorpe. The other player hit him high, Ike hit his legs, and the Indian crashed to the ground. Ike thought that the dazed and groggy Thorpe had finally been stopped, but he staggered to his feet and on the very next play barreled through the Army line for ten yards. The game ended with Carlisle winning 27–6. Ike limped slowly off the field, having suffered a wrenched knee.

Army bounded back the following week to hand Tufts a 15–6 defeat. Midway through the game Ike's weakened knee collapsed, and he had to be carried from the field on a stretcher. He spent several weeks in a hospital with his leg in a cast, and the injury proved so serious that his knee was never normal again. Ike's football career had come to an abrupt and tragic end. Army had lost one of its most promising backs, and the youthful cadet who would rather play football than eat or sleep was brokenhearted.

Eisenhower refused to become embittered over his own setback. During his remaining years at West Point, he stayed close to the game by helping to coach the Cullum Hall plebe team. Furthermore, the school officials were so impressed with his shortlived but spectacular football career that his name was imprinted on a special bronze tablet. It can still be seen today in the West Point gymnasium alongside tablets with the names of other Army athletic immortals.

Nearly fifty years after he left the Academy, Eisenhower emphasized the benefits that football can bring to the men who play the game. Speaking at a luncheon before the 1964 Rose Bowl game, he said, "Football is one game that is not going to lose its attraction. It is a contest that pits not only brawn, but brain, skill, discipline, and morale. In the Rose Bowl I will come to see young America training for greater problems. When I see these young people developing, I can have greater confidence in the future of our country." The former general told his audience that during the Second World War he had been required to relieve several officers on the battlefield because they lacked leadership qualities. "But," he added, "never did I have to relieve an officer who was an outstanding athlete."

During his long career as a military man and later as President, Eisenhower continued to follow the football fortunes of his beloved West Point. Even in the thick of battle far from home, he kept himself posted on how the Cadets fared each Saturday afternoon. Whenever an orderly brought news from the wireless of an Army victory, the general grinned broadly and his eyes shone brightly. After he moved into the White House, however, Eisenhower faced a rather embarrassing situation every time that Army played Navy. It is traditional for the President, as commander-in-chief, to be impartial when the service teams meet. But how could a lifelong Army man be expected to remain indifferent when his own alma mater took the field, especially against arch-rival Navy?

President Eisenhower managed to observe a formal neutrality during these crucial clashes. When he attended the games in person he dutifully sat on the Navy side for one of the halves. But there was no doubt where his sentiments lay. Before the 1958 game, for example, he sent a "personal best wishes" telegram to the Navy team. Then the old West Point grad telegrammed the Army team, explaining what he had told Navy and adding, "The requirements of neutrality are thus scrupulously observed. But over a span of almost half a century, on the day of The Game I have only one thought and only one song: 'On, brave old Army team.'"

2

On the Diamond

THE men who have served our country as President had various ambitions when they were young. Roscoe Drummond, the veteran news correspondent, gives the following account of President Eisenhower's reply to a question about his early ambitions.

"I remember one time when I was a boy in Kansas," Eisenhower said, "while I was in grade school, I think. I had a very good friend, and we got to talking about what we wanted to do when we grew up.

"I told him I had no doubt at all what I wanted. I said I wanted more than anything else in the whole world to be a baseball player, a good baseball player, a real professional — like Hans Wagner.

"Then I asked him: 'What do you want to be?'

"He answered, 'I want to be President of the United States.'

"The President reflected a moment, then added: 'Neither of us got our wish.' "

Eisenhower, however, probably came closer to being a good baseball player than any of the other men who lived in the White House. He played in the outfield on the Abilene High School nine and one year managed to lead his teammates in hitting and fielding. He also played a bit of local semi-pro ball before embarking on his military career.

Although he generally turned in a respectable performance, Ike played in one baseball game which he would have preferred to forget. That was when his high school outfit tangled with the Kansas University freshman team. Nearly the whole town of Abilene turned out to see how the local youngsters would fare against a college club. The game developed into a pitchers' battle, and Abilene held a surprising 1–0 lead going into the last inning. But then the tide of battle turned. With a runner on first base, the heaviest hitter on the Kansas team came to the plate. He slammed a hard line drive over second base.

Outfielder Eisenhower saw the ball coming, and he started moving in for it. But the ball carried high and deep into center field. Realizing he had misjudged the play, Ike stopped in his tracks and began running backward. Desperately he leaped for the ball, but it sailed over his head. By the time Ike picked up the ball and tossed it to the plate, the batter had rounded the bases with a home run. Kansas won the game, 2–1, and the dejected Eisenhower felt he had been the cause of his team's downfall.

Besides Eisenhower, a number of other Presidents played on the diamond. Although baseball as we know it did not develop until the 1840's, there is evidence that even our earliest Presidents played games that were the forerunners of the modern sport. George Washington was said to have played rounders, which called for batting, running, catching, and hurling. One account related that at Valley Forge he "sometimes throws and catches a ball for whole hours with his aide-de-camp." John Adams also enjoyed rounders, which was one of the few games permitted in staid New England.

A President who was very enthusiastic about baseball in his youth was William Howard Taft. He held down second base for a Cincinnati team known as the Mount Auburn club. "Big Bill" had powerful arms, and he wielded a strong bat at the plate. On the field he could scoop up the hot grounders and peg them accurately to first base. But Taft was not a fast runner, and this prevented him from becoming a first-rate player.

Before enrolling at Princeton, Woodrow Wilson briefly attended Davidson College in North Carolina, where he made the freshman baseball team. In one game the opposing team had two men on base, and the next batter drove a long fly deep into the outfield area that Wilson covered. Two runners appeared certain to score when Wilson jumped high in the air and made a spectacular catch of the ball. This apparently was the only occasion when Wilson was the hero of a game. Some of his performances on the diamond must have left much to be desired, for the Davidson captain was quoted as saying, "Wilson would be a good player if he weren't so damned lazy."

Wilson did not play baseball after he transferred to

Princeton, but he followed the sport closely and served as president of the Princeton Baseball Association. Later he studied law at Johns Hopkins University and had little time for any sport. In fact, seeing a game during that period of his life was such a treat that he wrote about it as follows to Ellen Axson, his future wife: "I have been suffering my one-time delight in baseball — which was my chief solace ten or twelve years ago . . . I like good company as much as I enjoy a good game of baseball, and, having both, I was immensely content, so to speak, though it was marvellously like wasting time, considering all I have to do before the close of the term."

The same thing happened to Herbert Hoover on the baseball diamond that had happened to him on the football field. He tried out for the Stanford nine but was not a good enough player to make the team. So, as in football, he became the team manager. "The job of manager," he explained, "consisted of arranging games, collecting the gate money and otherwise finding cash for equipment and uniforms." Hoover discovered that this job was harder work than playing on the team. When the team played at Santa Rosa, the receipts from the game were not large enough to buy the tickets home. Hoover had to canvass the Stanford parents in the town for donations to send the players back to school.

At Stanford there was no enclosed baseball park, so Hoover had to post assistants around the field to collect the twenty-five-cent entrance fee from the spectators. One day he observed that a bearded old gentleman had been allowed to enter free. The collector had lacked the nerve to demand a quarter from this distinguished guest. But Hoover could not ignore his duty, so he strode over to Benjamin Harrison and boldly asked the former President for the price of admission. "Mr. Harrison was cheerful about it," Hoover reported, "and bought also an advance ticket to the next week's game." He purchased his two tickets with a dollar bill and said he did not want the fifty cents change. However, the Stanford manager insisted that his school was not a charitable institution and that he must take his change. "Justice must occasionally be done even to ex-presidents," commented Hoover, "and I here record that he took two more tickets."

Franklin D. Roosevelt was another baseball enthusiast who failed to make his school team and had to settle for the job of manager. But at Groton he did play on a nine called the Bum Base Ball Boys, which he recorded "has no captain but is a republic and is made up of about the worst players in the school." In a game the BBBB played against CLLP (Carter's Little Liver Pills), Roosevelt admitted that "the only ball that I received, I nobly missed, and it landed biff! on my stomach, to the great annoyance of that intricate organ, and to the great delight of all present. The walls of my tummy caved in and a great panic ensued inside, similar to the Paris bonfire, only that a thunderbolt caused my catastrophe."

F.D.R.'s famous cousin, Theodore, also was unable to add baseball to his long list of sporting accomplishments.

He regretted this, and once, after watching his son Quentin play, he wrote, "I like to see Quentin practicing baseball. It gives me hopes that one of my boys will not take after his father in this respect, and will prove able to play the national game!" Theodore Roosevelt's poor eyesight and glasses prevented him from playing baseball. "I don't think that I should be afraid of anything except a baseball coming at me in the dark," he observed. Harry Truman was another President who had to wear glasses as a youth, and the neighborhood boys usually asked him to umpire their games.

Calvin Coolidge, on the other hand, could have played baseball, but he never was seriously interested in any game. A woman reporter once asked Coolidge if he had taken some part in athletics at college. "Yes, I did, an important part," he replied. Not a trace of a smile crossed his lips as he added sternly, "I held the stakes."

Coolidge was one of the few Presidents who did not care to attend baseball games either. His wife, however, was an avid baseball fan, and she rooted fervently for the Washington team when her husband was in the White House. At the opening game of the 1924 World Series between the Washington Senators and the New York Giants, the President rose to leave when the score was tied at the end of the ninth inning. Mrs. Coolidge clutched at her husband's coattails and begged him to sit back down. The President glumly returned to his seat and watched the rest of the game with bored indifference, while his wife helped cheer the Senators to an exciting victory. This was one of the incidents which caused Grace Coolidge to become known as the First Lady of Baseball. She attended games as often as possible, visited with the players in the dugout, and kept accurate records of the games on score cards. When she could not go to the park in person, Mrs. Coolidge followed the games on her radio, or slipped into the White House telegraph room to check the latest scores.

Although Abraham Lincoln watched baseball games between local Washington teams, the first President to view an inter-city game in the nation's capital was Andrew Johnson. In August 1865, he attended a two-game series between the Washington Nationals and the Philadelphia Athletics. It was played on the White Lot, a large tract of land to the south of the Executive Mansion. Many high government officials turned out for the festive occasion, and they sat near President Johnson in chairs that lined the field. The Athletics walloped the Nationals in the first game by an 87–12 score. But in the second game the hometown boys provided stronger competition and lost by a mere 34–19 margin. In spite of the beatings that were handed to their local team, the people of Washington seemed happy with their first inter-city competition. Members of both teams were entertained at the Willard Hotel, received by Congress, and welcomed at the White House by President Johnson.

Baseball games on the White Lot grew in popularity, and on Saturdays or holidays as many as ten thousand fans would cluster around the playing field and stand for two or three hours watching the teams play. One day James Garfield, who was then a congressman, was viewing a lengthy game. He was planning to catch a train for Chicago that afternoon, but he became so absorbed in the game that he forgot to check the time. A few minutes before the train was to depart a friend reminded him of the trip. Garfield ran to his carriage and ordered his coachman to gallop the horses down the crowded Washington streets to the station. Miraculously avoiding an accident, he reached the train with only a few seconds to spare.

Most of the twentieth century Presidents have been enthusiastic baseball fans. Warren Harding brought an expert knowledge of the game to Washington, for at one time he had played first base on the hometown club at Marion, Ohio, and also handled the team's finances. He frequently attended ball games in the national capital, and his critics claimed he spent more time poring over the box scores of the Washington baseball team than the Congressional Record. During Harding's administration the popular home run hero, Babe Ruth, was a guest at the White House several times.

Taft enjoyed baseball so much that he would sometimes attend two games in a single day, and once in Pittsburgh he refused to take a box seat and insisted on sitting in the bleachers. Hoover was another ardent fan, and he attended games long after he left the White House. On his eighty-seventh birthday the former President described himself as "the oldest living baseball fan," claiming that his allegiance to the game dated back to the time when he played sandlot ball at the age of ten.

Although crippled by a stroke while he was President, Wilson did not let this handicap stop him from attending baseball games in Washington. He watched from his car that had been driven onto the field and parked outside the right-field foul line. A spare player was stationed in front of the car to ward off any balls that might be headed in Wilson's direction. For Franklin D. Roosevelt, another baseball fan who was crippled, a special platform and railings were built at the Washington ball park. President Roosevelt could slip from his automobile onto the platform and pull himself up into his box with the help of the railings.

F.D.R. had a distinct preference for high-scoring games. "I am the kind of fan who wants to get plenty of action for his money," he explained. "I have some appreciation of a game which is featured by a pitchers' duel and results in a score of one to nothing. But I must confess that I get the biggest kick out of the biggest score — a game in which the batters pole the ball into the far corners of the field, the outfielders scramble, and men run the bases. In short, my idea of the best game is one that guarantees the fans a combined score of not less than fifteen runs, divided about eight to seven."

Because he was elected to four terms, Roosevelt had

the opportunity to throw out more balls at opening games of baseball seasons than any other President. This custom in which the Chief Executive kicked off the pennant races helped to establish baseball as the national pastime. No other sport is honored by the head of our government annually opening its season.

Taft was the President who inaugurated this famous custom at the beginning of the 1910 season. Newspaper accounts made much of the fact that Taft cheered loudly for the home team and stayed the full nine innings. "Washington has never seen such a baseball crowd," one paper reported, "as greeted the President when he entered the grounds just before the game opened. The immense crowd, numbering over 12,000, jumped to their feet as they made out the President and gave him a thundering round of cheers that drowned the band." Comparatively little newspaper space was devoted to a youngster named Walter Johnson who that afternoon pitched a one-hit shutout for the Senators. That was the first of Johnson's seven opening-day shutouts — a remarkable feat which still stands in the record books.

In 1912 Clark Griffith of the Washington team called at the White House and asked President Taft if he would make the practice of throwing out the first ball an annual function. "Why, sure, Griff," replied the agreeable Chief Executive. "I'll be glad to start the ball rolling."

Some eyebrows were raised when the ex-ballplayer of the Mount Auburn team accepted Griffith's offer. Tossing a ball in front of clicking cameras and a large noisy

crowd seemed to some citizens too trivial and undig-
nified to become a regular Presidential duty. But every
White House occupant since Taft has followed the practice. And, except for Coolidge, all of them apparently
have enjoyed that brief moment in April when they could
unlimber their arms and let go with a pitch.

Once, however, a President was forbidden to attend
the colorful opening game ceremonies. After the Japanese attacked Pearl Harbor in 1941, some outdoor events
were cancelled to prevent large crowds from being ex-
posed to possible bombings. Baseball officials inquired
about the government's attitude toward the ball parks
remaining open. President Roosevelt replied, "I honestly feel that it would be best for the country to keep
baseball going. . . . These players are a definite recrea-
tional asset to their fellow citizens — and that, in my
judgment, is thoroughly worthwhile." So the national
pastime was given the green light to continue providing
relaxation and pleasure for the American people. But
the Secret Service men, who guard the Chief Executive,
decided it was too great a security risk to permit the man
at the helm of the war effort to attend ball games.

Ironically, the President who helped to keep baseball
alive in wartime had to send a substitute to toss out the
first ball at the season opener.

3

In the Ring

THE man who lives in the White House is often in the thick of a fight. Every important step he takes, every new policy he launches may unleash an angry storm of criticism.

Many of our Presidents, when they were young, faced their opponents in physical combat instead of in the political arena. Powerfully built George Washington was said to be the best wrestler in his part of Virginia. Scrappy Andrew Jackson liked to tussle with the young bloods in North Carolina, even though his lean physique could not match his fighting spirit. "I could throw him three times out of four," declared one of Jackson's friends. "But he would never stay throwed. He was dead game and would never give up."

Zachary Taylor was a skilled wrestler and praised the sport as a healthful recreation. Calvin Coolidge wrestled during his Vermont boyhood, and William Allen White surmised that "his agility gave him equality with the biggest and the lustiest of the boys and the hired men in the village." Short, stocky Benjamin Harrison may not have been such a talented grappler, but once when an insane man broke into the White House, President Harrison jumped him and pinned his arms to his sides.

A strong and athletic youth, James Garfield battled "with the fury and tenacity of a bull-dog" against anyone who tried to take advantage of him. In his own neighborhood he earned the highly esteemed nickname of the "fighting boy." When he was sixteen and working on a canal boat, Garfield accidentally dropped a pole on a burly deck hand. Enraged and cursing, the sailor brushed aside the boy's apology and lunged at him. "I determined not to be whipped, but, if possible, to whip," recalled Garfield when he later described the incident. "Remaining perfectly still until he was almost upon me, I suddenly jumped aside, and as he passed I dealt him a terrible blow just back of and under his left ear." Stunned, the angry sailor fell prostrate to the deck. The captain of the boat urged Garfield to batter his victim while he was down, but the boy refused. "This fight," Garfield declared, "gave me much prestige with the rough men along the canal. I had whipped a man and was accorded a hero."

Another President who became a hero with his fists was Dwight Eisenhower. One day the neighborhood bully in Abilene, Kansas, jumped on Eisenhower's younger brother Roy. He threw him to the ground and rubbed his face in the mud. Dwight, whom the boys called "Ike," was only in grade school at the time. But he leaped to his brother's defense and stood up to the bully. A crowd of schoolboys gathered, and one of them put a chip on the bully's shoulder. No sooner had the roughneck dared young Ike to knock off the chip than he was staggered by a hard, fast punch that bloodied his nose. The startled boy swiftly backed away, and the honor of the Eisenhower family was avenged.

When Ike was only thirteen he took on one of the neighborhood's best fighters before a crowd of spectators in a vacant lot across from the Abilene city hall. The other youth was heavier, stronger, and much more experienced with his fists. Yet for two long hours Eisenhower battled his powerful foe. Ike's face was bruised and bleeding, and his eyes were swollen nearly shut, but he refused to back away. Despite all the punishment he took, somehow he managed to stay on his feet and keep trading punches. Only when the other fighter finally admitted that he could not beat Ike did the struggle end.

When Eisenhower went to West Point, his boyhood fighting techniques were refined. Trained instructors taught him to box scientifically and to use his arms and legs correctly. Meanwhile, back home in Abilene, a rugged young stalwart named Dirk Taylor was whipping all the local fighters. He was being acclaimed by some as the town champion. So when Eisenhower returned on a vacation to Abilene, the townsfolk clamored for a match to prove whether he or Taylor was the better man in the ring.

A bout was arranged in the basement of a department store, and excitement ran high as Abilene's two best fighters stripped for action. Taylor, a powerful man with rippling muscles, weighed about twenty pounds more than his opponent. But he was slow and awkward, and Eisenhower was able to dodge or block his punches. Early in the bout Taylor lunged off balance. Ike stepped in swiftly, caught Taylor's chin with a stiff left uppercut and followed with a strong right jab to his head. Taylor was left groggy and helpless after fighting less than three minutes, and the people of Abilene agreed that the West Point cadet was their champion boxer.

Some of the men who became President engaged in youthful fisticuffs that were not so heroic. A schoolmate recalled that when Ulysses S. Grant was about ten years old he won a fight by soundly kicking another boy in the leg. Grover Cleveland, while in his twenties, was walking down the street one night when he got into a heated political argument with one of his companions. The bitter exchange led to blows, and the two men swapped punch for punch in the middle of the street. One of Cleveland's biographers said that the most unusual feature about this fight was that "as the gentlemen were settling their argument in due and ancient form, they still pursued their northerly course." Apparently the scuffle ended in a draw, for the two battered battlers retired to a saloon to toast each other's health. Another President, Franklin Pierce, probably was not proud of his fighting days. Stories were told of how in college he started boisterous scraps which usually ended in damaging the furniture and causing bedlam for the authorities.

College was a place where William Howard Taft also

threw his weight around. One of the time-honored cus-
toms at Yale, where Taft was a student in the class of
1878, was the "rush" between the freshman and sophomore classes at the beginning of the fall term. The
"rush" would start with the freshmen marching from the
campus to the athletic field, nearly a mile away. They
would advance in as solid a body as possible, while fend-
ing off attacks from the sophomores along the way. At
the field there would be a vicious rough-and-tumble
scuffle in the mud, followed by wrestling bouts between
picked members of each class.

Powerful "Bill" Taft, who at that time weighed 225
pounds, was in the front line as the freshman class advanced toward the field. Determined that his classmates
must not be humiliated, Taft bowled over all challengers
with a mighty onslaught. One of the sophomores who
was trapped in his path said the experience was "like
that of being plowed over by a landslide." After the on-
rushing freshmen reached the water-soaked field, Taft
wallowed and scuffled gloriously in the muddy free-for-
all. Then he led his classmates as they fought their way
back to the campus amidst raucous cheers of victory.

Taft also was selected to represent his class in one of
the wrestling bouts. Arthur T. Hadley, an upperclass-
man who later became president of Yale, recalled, "I
saw Taft strip and get into the ring, and I knew from
the way the sophomore smote the earth that something
had happened to him. Taft must have made him think
a house had tumbled on him. After the performance I

shook hands with the victor and congratulated him, inwardly thanking my stars that I had not been the other fellow."

The mammoth lad from Cincinnati went on to become the heavyweight wrestling champion at Yale. He held this crown for two years. Hadley later remarked that "the manner in which 'Bill' Taft got into the heavyweight wrestling and the way he stroked the freshman crew satisfied me that he was the man for about anything, even for running the country."

On one occasion shortly after his college days, Taft made use of his physical strength to defend his father's name. Lester A. Rose, a newspaperman, had written a vicious and scandalous article about Taft's father, who was a prominent judge. Taft was warned that Rose was a strong and rugged fighter, but this did not frighten the future President. He approached the man on a busy Cincinnati street corner, asked him his name to be sure he had the right person, and then proceeded to give him a sound thrashing. The Cincinnati *Commercial* contained a half-column article about the fight under the headlines: "A Sensationist Punished. Will Taft served Lester A. Rose. A Sound Beating Cleverly Administered."

Another President who as a youth won acclaim for his remarkable strength was Abraham Lincoln. The rugged railsplitter could lift four hundred pounds with ease, and once he was said to have lifted six hundred pounds. A neighbor recalled he walked away with a pair of huge logs that three robust men had doubted they could even pick up. Another witness said he could "sink an ax deeper than any man I ever saw." In wrestling, which was probably Lincoln's favorite sport, he took great delight in pinning back the shoulders of everyone who challenged him.

In July of 1831, when Lincoln was twenty-two and still, in his own words, "a piece of floating driftwood," he went to visit his father in Coles County, Illinois. In Cumberland County, which joined Coles, a tough young buck named Dan Needham was the champion wrestler. As soon as word of Lincoln's prowess reached Needham, he boasted, "I can fling that young upstart any day in the week." Abe accepted the challenge, and the two rivals met in a wrestling match at Wabash Point.

Both the sinewy, raw-boned contestants stood six feet four, and, according to Carl Sandburg, resembled prairie panthers. But young Abe was much stronger than his opponent and easily pinned his shoulders to the ground. Needham went down so swiftly that his pride was stung. Angrily he threatened to turn the wrestling match into a fist fight. Lincoln chuckled and replied that if throwing his man was not convincing enough, he might have to give him a thrashing too. Flabbergasted by the casual manner of his foe, Needham decided he had better call it quits while he still could. The disgruntled loser thrust out his hand and muttered, "Well, I'll be damned."

Soon after this incident Lincoln settled down in New Salem, Illinois, where he worked as a clerk in the general store owned by Denton Offut. Before Lincoln had been there long, he was taunted by the young bloods of the village to prove whether he could live up to the tales they had heard about his athletic ability. Three contests were arranged to show the stuff that young Abe was made of. First he was to run a race with a fleet-footed man from Wolf. Then he was expected to wrestle with a rough grappler from Little Grove. After that, he was to fight a rugged battler from Sand Ridge. Abe reluctantly agreed to accept these challenges as his initiation into the New Salem fraternity.

The foot-racer from Wolf never was able to pass the speedy clerk. The short, heavy wrestler from Little Grove charged like a bull, but Lincoln caught him by the nape of the neck, twisted him heels over head, and tossed him to the ground with a bone-jarring thud. Then Lincoln straightened up and called to the crowd, "Bring on your fighter from Sand Ridge. I can lick you all if you give me ten minutes between fights." But by then the youths were thoroughly impressed that the new clerk at the dry-goods store could do all that was claimed for him. Calling off any further exhibitions, they crowded around to shake his hand.

Lincoln's most ardent admirer was his employer, Denton Offut. He enthusiastically boasted that his clerk could "outrun, outlift, outwrestle, and throw down any man in Sangamon County." One Saturday afternoon Offut strutted back and forth in front of his store, hailing passersby with extravagant claims about the manly prowess of his employee and waving a handful of silver which he offered to bet on him. Lincoln was inside the store at the time, and when he heard Offut crowing about him he hurried outside and tried in vain to quiet his boss. Bill Clary, who ran the saloon next door, also heard Offut's boasts. He gladly accepted his bet with the blunt warning that the fellow on whom he staked his money would slaughter the gangling clerk. The saloon-keeper pinned his hopes on an exceptionally powerful, well-developed specimen of manhood named Jack Armstrong.

Armstrong was the leader of the Clary's Grove boys, who lived about four miles from New Salem. They were a pack of hard-fighting, hot-tempered rowdies who measured the worth of a man only in terms of his courage and strength. Armstrong had earned the right to bark orders to the pack after he had proven in combat that he was the roughest and toughest of the lot. This square-built hulk of a man had vanquished everyone who had dared to test him, and on his oxlike shoulders Clary felt that his bet was secure.

Spectators came from as far as fifty miles away to watch the struggle that was to take place on a vacant lot next to Offut's store. The Clary's Grove boys turned out in mass, and they placed bets of money, knives, trinkets, and whiskey on their contender.

The two goliaths, stripped to the waist, eyed each other cautiously. Armstrong's strategy was to move in close where he could put to advantage his steellike torso and shoulders. The taller and lankier Lincoln, weighing fifteen pounds less than his two-hundred-pound opponent, counted on his agility and longer reach to offset Armstrong's brute force. The wrestlers clenched, broke, and clenched again, each trying to grapple the other man to the ground.

With his long arms Lincoln generally managed to keep Armstrong from getting a punishing hold. Slowly he wore down the resistance of the Clary's Grove champion. Armstrong began breathing in short gasps, and he started snorting oaths at the clever opponent who was frustrating him. Lincoln patiently bided his time until the chance came for him to apply a painful headlock. As Abe's viselike arms tightened around his foe's head, the irate Armstrong stamped heavily with his bootheel on the instep of Lincoln's foot.

Infuriated by this foul trick, Lincoln gathered all his strength for one mighty effort. With muscles tense he lifted Armstrong by the throat. Holding him high in the air, he shook him like a rag and then slammed him heavily to the ground. Armstrong lay flat on his back, dazed and breathless.

Shocked at the sight of their fallen hero, the Clary's Grove boys began swarming around Lincoln and shouting curses at the victorious clerk. As the angry mob pushed in, Lincoln backed against the store wall and announced he was willing to fight them all one at a time. But by then Armstrong was back on his feet. Shoving through the crowd, he grasped Lincoln's hand.

"He's the best feller that ever broke into this settlement," declared the beaten man.

From that time on Jack Armstrong and his family were close and loyal friends of Lincoln. Moreover, the young clerk became the new hero of the Clary's Grove boys and the other youths in Sangamon County. They called on him to judge their cockfights, gander pulls, and horse races, to referee their contests, and to settle their arguments. Abe Lincoln became their frontier idol, and these rough-hewn bucks from Clary's Grove were among the first hero-worshipers of the man who was to become the most beloved figure in our nation's history.

The Clary's Grove boys believed their new champion was unbeatable as a wrestler, and he proved, except in one instance, that they were correct. When Lincoln led a company of volunteers from Sangamon County to fight the Black Hawk Indians in 1832, soldiers from all parts of Illinois challenged him without success. Finally a well-known wrestler from Union County by the name of Lorenzo Thompson asked for the chance to take on Captain Lincoln. A championship match, with the winner taking two out of three falls, was arranged. Lincoln's fans enthusiastically bet everything they could lay their hands on — cash, whiskey, knives, hats, blankets, and even tomahawks.

After the two soldiers had clenched and separated a few times, Abe looked at his friends in the crowd and said, "Boys, this is the most powerful man I ever had hold of." For a while the men battled on even terms, and then Thompson threw Lincoln with a "crotch hoist" for the first fall. Back on their feet again, the two wrestlers tugged and twisted and grappled with all their might. Then suddenly Abe dropped to the ground, dragging Thompson down with him.

The Lincoln rooters shouted that the second fall was a "dog-fall," or a draw, while Thompson's backers claimed their man had downed the railsplitter for a second and final time. Charging foul play, Lincoln's friends swarmed around the wrestlers and threatened to settle the dispute in their own free-for-all manner. But Abe faced the crowd and shouted, "Boys, give up your bets. If this man hadn't thrown me fairly, he could." His loyal supporters never would concede that their man had lost the match, but years later Lincoln admitted Thompson was the only man who had ever thrown him and added, "He could have thrown a grizzly bear."

Lincoln launched his political career by mixing a bit of wrestling with his oratory. His first stump speech was made at Pappville, a village eleven miles west of Springfield, following a public sale in which an auctioneer had disposed of hogs, bulls, and steers. On this occasion, in 1832, Lincoln was a candidate for the state legislature. Just as he stepped up to begin his maiden speech, the young politician observed a ruffian attacking one of his friends in the crowd. Hurriedly Lincoln descended from the platform. Edging his way through the crowd, he grabbed the bully by the neck and the seat of his pants and heaved him about ten feet for a thumping fall. Having done what he considered his duty, he casually mounted the platform again and began his speech.

While Lincoln won more fame than any other President as a wrestler, Theodore Roosevelt was the number one boxer. The weak, sickly boy who eventually developed into a vigorous, all-around sportsman became interested in boxing when he was twelve years old. This happened after he had returned from a summer camp where two of the other boys had taken advantage of their puny, nearsighted companion by shoving and punching him. "The worst feature," Roosevelt recalled in his autobiography, "was that when I finally tried to fight them I discovered that either one simply could not only handle me with easy contempt, but handle me so as not to hurt me much and yet to prevent my doing any damage whatever in return."

Roosevelt continued, "The experience taught me what probably no amount of good advice could have taught me. I made up my mind that I must try to learn so that I would not again be put in such a helpless position; and having become quickly and bitterly conscious that I did not have the natural powers to hold my own . . . I started to learn to box."

His first boxing instructor was John Long, a former prizefighter. Teddy was a painfully slow and awkward pupil, and he admitted that he worked two or three years before there was any noticeable improvement.

The frail lad took plenty of punishment from the other students, but he kept coming back for his boxing lessons and exercising every day in a small gymnasium outfitted in his home. Then one day he surprised his boxing instructor by winning a pewter mug in a class tournament. Years later Roosevelt remarked that "it happened that I was pitted against a couple of reedy striplings who were even worse than I was." Even so, the pewter mug became one of his most prized possessions.

When Theodore Roosevelt was seventeen and went away to Harvard, he still was far from being a robust youth. But at college Teddy went in for both boxing and wrestling. This was partly because he liked them as sports, and, as he explained, "it was even more because I intended to be a middling decent fellow, and I did not intend that anyone should laugh at me with impunity because I was decent." To add the final touch of assurance that no one would laugh at him for being "decent," young Roosevelt wore a pair of reddish sideburns that made him look rugged.

Owen Wister, author of *The Virginian,* said the first time he saw Roosevelt was one afternoon in November 1878 in the Harvard gymnasium. The future President, who was then a junior, was boxing with a senior. Wister recalled that at the end of one round "time" had been called and Roosevelt stopped fighting. But the senior did not hear the signal, and, according to Wister, "he landed a very palpable hit on Mr. Roosevelt's nose, which bled immediately and copiously." A loud hiss rose from the angered spectators who knew that "time" had been called.

Teddy whirled about, and, getting the attention of the crowd, called out: "It's all right! It's all right! He didn't hear the call." Smiling amiably he then shook his opponent's hand, and the audience responded with a mighty roar of applause. "You may imagine what ardent champions Mr. Roosevelt had during the final round," said Wister. "Nobody cared about whether the senior showed the more science or not. The judges, if I remember, decided that he did."

Although he wrote his family that he sparred daily in the gymnasium, during his college days Roosevelt did not become a first-rate boxer. In those years he was handicapped by a slender physique, as well as by a short reach and the poor eyesight that plagued him all his life. But in spite of these drawbacks, he entered the Harvard lightweight championship tournament in his junior year. After winning an initial bout, Teddy was pitted against a senior who was stronger and had a longer reach. Because of his bad eyes he knew that in-fighting gave him the only chance to win. During the first round the senior let his opponent move in and draw first blood, but after that he held Roosevelt at arm's length and landed frequent blows. The senior won the bout, and the *New York Times* in a brief item said that the winner spent most of the match "punishing Roosevelt severely." But the victor later admitted that Roosevelt was "far more

scientific" and, "given good eyes, he would have defeated me easily."

A few years after graduating from college Roosevelt
became a rancher in the Dakota Badlands. The arduous conditions of the Old West hardened and toughened
Roosevelt's body, and it was during these years that he
first really adopted the "Strenuous Life." His wrestling
was confined to staying on top of bucking broncos and
struggling with stubborn steers, but on one occasion he
put his training as a boxer to good use. This was when
a gun-wielding cowpuncher approached Roosevelt in a
hotel bar and sarcastically called him "Four Eyes" because he wore glasses. The ruffian drew his guns and
ordered "Four Eyes" to buy everyone in the bar a drink.

Roosevelt meekly replied, "Well, if I must, I must,"
and he walked up to the bar as if to order the drinks.
Then suddenly he wheeled around, and his right fist shot
out at the cowpuncher's jaw. He followed with a solid
left and then another stinging right. The troublemaker
tumbled to the floor, firing both guns into the ceiling as
he fell. Roosevelt jumped on him, and, with his knees
on his victim's chest, disarmed him in a hurry. The
crowd of amazed onlookers then helped him hog-tie the
unhappy fellow and put him in an outhouse.

While he was a police commissioner in New York City,
Roosevelt encouraged the formation of boxing clubs in
the slums to provide a healthy outlet for the energies of
the boys who lived there. "In the same way," Roosevelt
later wrote, "I have always regarded boxing as a first-

class sport to encourage in the Young Men's Christian Association. I do not like to see young Christians with shoulders that slope like a champagne bottle."

Later, while he was governor of New York, Roosevelt seemed to do an about-face when he approved a bill that outlawed prizefighting in his state. But he explained his action with the comment that "the only objection I have to the prize ring is the crookedness that has attended its commercial development . . . I shall always maintain that boxing contests themselves make good healthy sport."

Governor Roosevelt kept himself in fighting trim by boxing twice a week with Mike Donovan, a former middleweight champion. The first time he faced the governor in the ring Donovan led with a light left jab and followed with a soft right punch that landed like a love-tap on his chin. At that point Teddy indignantly stopped the match and ordered Donovan to begin hitting hard. Donovan agreed, and soon both men began swapping leather as if the championship belt were at stake. One of Roosevelt's solid right smashes "jarred me down to the heels," reported Donovan. "I realized from that moment that the governor was no ordinary amateur. If I took chances with him I was endangering my reputation."

Roosevelt continued his torrid matches with Donovan after he moved into the White House. On March 3, 1905, the evening before Roosevelt's inauguration for his full four-year term, the President and Donovan had a bruising ten-round go. The former middleweight champion recalled that Teddy was as happy as a schoolboy when he stripped for the match. "Now, Mike," he said, "we must have a good bout this evening. It will brighten me for tomorrow, which will be a trying day."

The President took on other well-known boxers, and the White House gymnasium came to resemble a private Madison Square Garden. Teddy could hold his own in these exhausting workouts. "Had President Roosevelt come to the prize ring instead of the political arena," observed Donovan, "it is my conviction that he would have been successful. The man is a born fighter. It's in his blood." Unfortunately, Roosevelt's boxing in the White House came to an abrupt end when an Army captain landed a blow that caused him to lose the sight of his left eye.

But the vigorous President took this serious injury in his stride and turned instead to wrestling. A few years earlier, when he had been governor of New York, he had grappled several times with a champion wrestler. In fact, the notion of wrestling in the executive mansion at Albany had led to a humorous rift between the governor and the state comptroller. The officer who held the state's purse strings stubbornly refused to pay the bill for Roosevelt's wrestling mat. The comptroller ruled, according to Roosevelt, "that I could have a billiard-table, billiards being recognized as a proper Gubernatorial amusement, but that a wrestling-mat symbolized something unusual and unheard of and could not be permitted." Refusing to be discouraged, Roosevelt paid for the mat himself.

In addition to his regular wrestling bouts in the White House, the President decided to take up jujitsu. He hired Japanese wrestlers to instruct him in this Oriental sport three times a week. Writing to his son Kermit in 1904, Roosevelt said, "I am not the age or the build one would think to be whirled lightly over an opponent's head and batted down on a mattress without damage. But they are so skillful that I have not been hurt at all." Then he added wryly, "My throat is a little sore, because once when one of them had a strangle hold I also got hold of his windpipe and thought I could perhaps choke him off before he could choke me. However, he got ahead."

Once Roosevelt staged a match between a professional Washington wrestler with whom he worked and one of his jujitsu instructors. The President decided to referee the match himself, but he obviously wanted the American wrestler to prove that his style was superior. The Japanese, however, easily tossed the American over his head and bounced him on the floor. Dazed and angry, the wrestler then broke the rules and tackled his opponent from the rear, pinning him to the floor so he could not budge. At this point the stanch patriotism of Roosevelt came to the fore, and he declared the American the victor. The confused jujitsu artist was led away, muttering that he could have smashed the arms and legs of his burly foe if the President had given him the chance.

The professional boxers and wrestlers were sorry to see Roosevelt leave the White House. He was their kind of man; they virtually idolized him. And Teddy understood and respected them. Besides Mike Donovan, his friends from the ring included Battling Nelson, Bob Fitzsimmons, and the great John L. Sullivan. Boxers called often at the White House, and the President made senators and Cabinet members wait outside his office for hours while he chatted with them. Fitzsimmons once presented the President a penholder made out of a horseshoe, and before Roosevelt set out on his hunting expedition to Africa, Sullivan gave him a gold-mounted rabbit's foot. Later Roosevelt said of the rabbit's foot: "I carried it through my African trip; and I certainly had good luck."

The way the boxers felt about their companion who had done so well in the main event at 1600 Pennsylvania Avenue was summed up in a remark Sullivan made to reporters in 1910: ". . . If you want to quote me on anything special, just say that John L. Sullivan thinks the Creator played a low-down trick on the Irish when he made Roosevelt a Dutchman."

4

On the Hunting Trail

CHASING the elusive fox was the favorite sport of George Washington. Like the other Virginia plantation owners, the Father of our Country spent many happy hours riding to the hounds and enjoying the companionship of the hunting fraternity.

During the season when the planters followed the scent of Reynard, Mount Vernon was the center of gay social activities. From near and far came friends and relatives, whose visits often lasted several weeks. Washington and his wife Martha were gracious hosts, and they entertained their guests in the lavish manner that was typical of Southern hospitality.

Weather permitting, there usually was a hunt three times a week. The hunters rose before dawn, and breakfast was served by candlelight. By sunrise the riders were in the saddle, eager to follow the yelping dogs. The hunt might last for several hours, with the riders racing at reckless speed through the tangled woods and over the gullies and fences. After the chase the party would return to the mansion house, where toasts would be raised to the boldest rider, the most gallant horse, the leading dog, and even the fleet-footed fox.

Cost was never spared in preparing for the elaborate hunts. Washington had the finest clothes, the strongest horses, and the best hounds that money could buy. He wore a blue coat, scarlet waistcoat, buckskin breeches, and velvet cap, and he carried a whip with a long thong. Usually he rode to the chase on Blueskin, a swift animal that had great endurance in a long run. Washington was particularly fond of this horse, which he named for the dark iron-gray color that gave its coat a bluish hue. Always providing a strong ride, Blueskin would return from a hunt with its nostrils distended and its coat lathered with sweat.

Washington kept a large pack of excellent hounds, and he inspected his kennels along with his stables every morning and evening when he was at Mount Vernon. His hounds were of such fine quality that "if one leading dog should lose the scent, another was at hand immediately to recover it, and thus when in full cry, to use a racing phrase, you might cover the pack with a blanket." From their owner these hounds acquired such fascinating names as Truelove, Mopsey, Pilot, Musick, Bell Tongue, Sweetlips, Trueman, and Duchess. When Washington was away from Mount Vernon during the Revolutionary War, his number of good dogs was greatly reduced. After the war his friend the Marquis de Lafayette sent the general a gift of some French staghounds to help restore his pack. One of these hounds was so large that Washington's adopted grandson rode him around the plantation.

No one enjoyed the Mount Vernon hunts more than the host himself. G. W. Parke Custis, Washington's adopted grandson, wrote, "There were roads cut through the woods in various directions, by which the aged or timid hunters, and ladies, could enjoy the exhilarating cry, without risk of life or limb, but Washington rode gaily up to his hounds, through all the difficulties and dangers of the grounds on which he hunted . . . always in at the death, and yielding to no man the honor of the brush . . ."

In his diaries Washington frequently referred to his hunting experiences. Sometimes he told of success, such as in this entry: "Went a Huntg . . . and killed a Dog Fox after treeing him in 35 mins . . ." Other references, such as "went a hunting, but catched nothing" and "found a Fox and run it 6 hours and then lost," recorded his failures. At times the unexpected occurred, such as when Washington reported, "Went a Hunting . . . catched a Rakoon but never found a Fox."

Washington sometimes would catch his fox in half an hour or he might run it nearly the whole day in vain. A certain black fox proved especially troublesome. It was chased seven or eight times but always eluded the frustrated hunters. Often the chase ended with the weary fox climbing a tree to escape. One of Washington's most remarkable hunts involved a fox that twice took to the trees. On that occasion he recorded: "Went a hunting after breakfast and found a Fox at Muddy Hole and killed her (it being a Bitch), after a chase of better than two hours, and treeing her twice, the last of which times she fell dead out of the Tree after being therein sevl. minutes apparently well."

Besides tracking down foxes, Washington hunted the other wild game that abounded in the virgin forests and waters of colonial America. On various outings he sighted along the barrel of his gun at deer, buffaloes, turkeys, pheasants, and ducks. One of his most successful hunting adventures occurred during an expedition that he led into the Ohio Territory in 1770. He reported in his journal of that trip that one day his party "killed five wild turkeys," and three days later they "saw innumerable quantities of turkeys and many deer watering and browsing on the south shore, some of which we killed." The high point in markmanship came when the travelers took a day off from their journey and "went a hunting; killed five buffaloes and wounded some others, three deer, etcra."

Washington liked to go "a ducking" in the creeks and coves of his plantation. But he gave strict orders that others were not to hunt ducks on his property without his permission. One morning when the Mount Vernon proprietor was riding, his eye caught the flutter of wings above one of the coves. Suddenly the crack of a rifle shot sounded through the bushes, and a bird fell from the sky. Whirling his horse around, Washington headed at full speed toward the cove.

The poacher, who was shoving off in a canoe, heard the horse approaching and raised his gun. "Stop or I shoot!" he commanded as Washington rode into sight. But the angry plantation owner kept galloping toward the man. Dashing his horse headlong into the water, he swiftly lunged for the gun and tossed it aside. Then he caught the frightened poacher by the scruff of the neck, pulled him out of the boat, and beat him until he promised never to set foot again on his property.

In the early days of our country's history hunting was a way of life, as well as a sport, for the people who lived on the frontier and in rural areas. When they were young, a number of our Presidents took to the woods and streams to help provide the meat and fowl that were needed for the family meals. Even those who came from wealthy homes were taught to hunt as a means of developing self-reliance.

A story was told of how Thomas Jefferson was given a gun when he was ten years old and instructed by his father to go into the woods and not come home until he had killed some game. Young Jefferson searched far and wide, but he had no luck in finding a suitable victim. Finally he stumbled across a wild turkey that was trapped in a pen. He tied the turkey to a tree with his garter, shot it, and then carried it home over his shoulder to lay at the feet of his proud parent.

Pioneer settlers took great pride in accurate marksmanship. When James Buchanan was a boy, the forests of Pennsylvania resounded with the crack of his rifle. He learned how to gauge his shots at the moving targets that darted among the trees. Young Buchanan could handle his weapon so deftly that he considered it a disgrace to go home with a squirrel unless the bullet had been sent directly through its head.

Andrew Jackson was another President who excelled at shooting. As a backwoods youth he foraged for game in the Carolina wilderness. There he acquired the accurate aim which saved his life when he later became involved in duels. His superb marksmanship also came in handy on happier occasions. When Jackson became a circuit lawyer in Tennessee and rode long distances between the county courts, he always took with him his shotgun and very often his hounds. Friends along the route would ask him to join in a deer chase or fox hunt, and if he was not too pressed for time he gladly accepted their invitations.

Jackson often would dismount on these trips to participate in local shooting matches. The prizes might be turkeys or quarters of beef or venison. Following such matches, the young lawyer usually rode off with his saddlebags stuffed with fresh meat. Even when he grew old, Jackson was a better rifleman than most men half his age. After he had left the White House and was past seventy, he could still drop a squirrel or behead a wild turkey with his old flintlock rifle.

Abraham Lincoln also was reputed to be an expert rifleman, but he was not fond of hunting. One of his childhood recollections was of a flock of wild turkeys that approached his family's new cabin in Indiana. His father was not at home, and Abe, then only eight years old, received permission from his mother to use his father's gun. The boy stood inside the cabin and, shooting through a crack, brought down one of the birds. But instead of being impressed by his own marksmanship, young Lincoln was fascinated by the beauty of the bird he had killed. From that time on it was said that he never pulled a trigger on any large game.

Another President who disliked hunting was Ulysses S. Grant. Although he enjoyed shooting at targets, he was so sensitive to pain that he could not bring himself to destroy any form of wildlife. Grant had no appetite for fowl, and he once remarked that "I never could eat anything that goes on two legs." During the Mexican War he watched his officer friends come into camp laden with ducks and turkeys. Once he tried to take part in one of their turkey hunts, but after reaching the hunting grounds he simply stood and watched with awe the flight of the birds. Grant returned to the camp thoroughly convinced that he would never become even a mediocre hunter. Years later the military President recalled, "Twice in my life I killed wild animals, and I have regretted both acts ever since."

Grover Cleveland, on the other hand, never regretted his many delightful hunting excursions. "I am an enthusiast in my devotion to hunting and fishing," he explained. ". . . So far as my attachment to outdoor sports may be considered a fault, I am utterly incorrigible and shameless." His enthusiasm extended beyond merely answering the call of the wild; Cleveland became a first-rate authority on both hunting and fishing. After his retirement from public office, he wrote articles on these outdoor sports for such publications as *Collier's, Saturday Evening Post, Independent,* and *Woman's Home Companion.* In 1906 some of his articles were published in book form under the title *Fishing and Outdoor Sketches.*

Hunting took Cleveland to various parts of the East. He shot ducks on Chesapeake Bay and in the Carolinas, stalked deer in the Adirondacks, aimed at shorebirds on Cape Cod, and tramped for quail and rabbit near the home where he lived in retirement at Princeton, New Jersey. Some hunters, Cleveland admitted, would never pursue the lowly rabbit, but he considered that this was "pure affectation and nonsense." After he left the White House, the former President wrote in one of his articles that the rabbit was an "entirely suitable member of the game community." He made it clear that he was referring to the ". . . plain, little, everyday plebeian rabbits — sometimes appropriately called 'cotton-tails.' I am not ashamed of their pursuit," continued Cleveland, "and I count it by no means bad skill to force them by a successful shot to a topsy-turvey pause when at their best speed."

Ducks were high on the list of Cleveland's favorite targets. He would sit patiently in the duckblind from sunrise to sunset, waiting hours at a time for a good crack at a low-flying mallard. Stories were circulated about his many hunting successes, and on one occasion it was reported that his five-man party had killed five hundred ducks in four days. Hotly denying this claim, Cleveland set the record straight with a statement that he and his party had brought down *only* about 125 birds. While he was a strict believer in the game regulations, the President generally refused to leave a duckblind until he had bagged the legal limit. In those rare instances when another man knocked down a bird he had missed, Cleveland admitted he was "somewhat distressed." "This we call 'wiping the eye,' " he said, "but I have always thought the sensation caused . . . justified calling it 'gouging the eye.' "

Hunting was regarded by Cleveland as a highly technical science. Before going after shorebirds, for example, he made elaborate preparations, calculated the direction of the wind and other weather conditions, and practiced imitating the necessary bird calls. His duck-hunting excursions were just as carefully plotted. On one trip he protested strongly when the decoys were placed to the windward side of his hunting party. Cleveland maintained this would cause the ducks to spot the hunters before they saw the decoys. "We killed a few ducks through much tribulation," he conceded, "but the irritation of knowing that many good opportunities were lost by our improper location more than overbalances all the satisfaction of our slight success." The next day Cleveland made certain that the decoys were placed to the leeward side, and his theory seemed to be vindicated when twice as many ducks were shot.

Cleveland had less success bringing down quail. He

frankly admitted, "I do not assume to be competent to give instructions in quail shooting. I miss too often to undertake such a role." The former President believed the problem of many quail hunters, including himself, was shooting too quickly when a bird rises. The quail's flight seems more rapid than it actually is, and the hunter instinctively pulls the trigger before taking careful aim. Cleveland found it hard to practice what he preached when he passed along the following good advice to fellow quail hunters: "When the bird gets up, if you chew tobacco spit over your shoulder before you shoot."

A few years after Cleveland left the White House, the man Mark Hanna referred to as "that damned cowboy" became President. Theodore Roosevelt was one of the most remarkable hunters of all time, and his many exciting expeditions were widely publicized throughout the world. Whenever the rough-and-ready Chief Executive picked up his guns and departed for some remote hunting grounds, newspaper editors knew that the unpredictable Teddy would make front-page news. The President himself helped to immortalize these experiences by faithfully recording his numerous hunting adventures in a series of popular books.

Roosevelt's lengthy career as a hunter reflected his lifelong search for experiences that were new and different. As a young man he rode to the hounds on Long Island, but he came to regard this type of hunting as too tame and commonplace. When Teddy traveled to the

Badlands of North Dakota, he would not rest until he had bagged a buffalo. His spirit of adventure took him to British Columbia for caribou, to Louisiana for bear, to Colorado for lions and cougars, to the Shoshone Mountains for elk, to the Bitterroot country of Montana and Idaho for moose. After he stepped down from the Presidency, he departed in 1909 for a long, arduous expedition into the heart of Africa in quest of every available species of animal life. In 1913 he undertook his final and most hazardous adventure — a trip into the wilderness sections of Brazil to navigate the seldom-traveled River of Doubt and to shoot such jungle game as tapirs and jaguars. The former President nearly died from disease and infection on this expedition, and he never again recovered his full vigor and robust health. Even so, Roosevelt felt no self-pity about his ordeal. Later he looked back wistfully on his harrowing Brazilian journey as his "last chance to be a boy."

Teddy, however, did not try to be a daredevil on the hunting trails. He rarely if ever took unusual risks just for the thrills they produced. His willingness to live dangerously and undergo severe hardships stemmed instead from his great desire to achieve the hunting goals he had set for himself. Once his mind was made up to stalk certain game, nothing short of the wrath of heaven could stop him.

This driving determination was displayed when he first arrived in the Badlands in 1883 and asked for a guide to help him track down buffalo. The rugged frontiersmen laughed out loud at his request. They could not believe that a bespectacled dude from the East who wore fancy corduroy pants was seriously interested in pursuing dangerous game. But Roosevelt persisted, and he finally obtained his guide. After luckless days of getting lost, cutting open his forehead, being caught in torrential downpours, getting punctured by cactus spires, losing his horse, and running out of food and water, Teddy finally got his buffalo. In the midst of his troubles one night Roosevelt turned over in rain-soaked blankets and exclaimed to his guide, "By Godfrey but this is fun!" Needless to say, when the astonished guide returned with his patron to the frontier settlement, the impression of the Eastern dude changed radically.

Roosevelt acquired two ranches in the Badlands country, and he spent some of the happiest years of his life there. In 1884 he wrote, "I grow very fond of this place, and it certainly has a desolate, grim beauty of its own, that has a certain fascination for me." In addition to raising cattle, he used his ranches as bases for hunting trips in search of deer, antelope, coyotes, foxes, and more buffalo. Writing to his sister about one of these trips, he said, "For the last week I have been fulfilling a boyish ambition of mine — that is, I have been playing at frontier hunter in good earnest, having been off entirely alone, with my horse and rifle on the prairie. I wanted to see if I could not do perfectly well without a guide, and I succeeded beyond my expectations. I shot a couple of antelope and a deer, and missed a great many more. I felt as absolutely free as a man could feel . . . and I enjoyed the trip to the utmost."

After Roosevelt left the West and became deeply involved in politics, his hunting expeditions provided a healthful change of pace. Leaving behind the crowded calendar of official duties and getting back on the trail worked as a tonic for his frayed nerves and tired spirit. Invariably he returned to his desk refreshed and relaxed, eager to tackle the problems at hand. And Roosevelt always was ready to talk about his most recent hunting exploits to anyone who would listen.

One expedition, however, Teddy enjoyed less than the others. In 1902, while he was President, he traveled to the Yazoo delta in Mississippi to hunt bear. Afterward the newspapers said that Roosevelt's trip had been a failure. For four days a guide had led him on spirited rides through briers and tangles that covered the President's face and hands with scratches, but all of the big bear managed to stay out of sight. Once, however, Roosevelt had a chance at a small brown bear, but when he saw that it was undersized he refused to shoot. A political cartoonist later sketched this incident, and, as a result, the original "Teddy bear" was born.

When Roosevelt moved into the White House, the State Dining Room took on a new appearance. Stuffed heads of animals shot by the President were hung on the walls. Mrs. Eleanor Roosevelt once said that it was not a particularly pleasant experience to eat with "Uncle Ted" and suddenly look up to see the eyes of a stuffed moose or some other animal glaring down at the diners. But an adoring public saw nothing wrong in their President turning a staid dining room into an exhibition hall for his hunting trophies. His hunting exploits were, after all, visible symbols of qualities which Americans held dear — courage, initiative, self-reliance, perseverance.

Many people were fascinated with Roosevelt because this very capable President was at heart an overgrown adolescent. Some of his followers, however, feared that his youthful exuberance might someday get him into trouble. So from time to time the President promised his friends that he would take no unnecessary chances on his hunting trips. He made such a promise before leaving on a trip to Oklahoma to shoot wolves and rabbits.

Roosevelt's cowboy guide in Oklahoma was known far and wide as the man who "caught 'em alive." He would chase wolves around the prairie all day until they would literally drop from exhaustion. Then he would hop off his horse and seize the animal in his hands. Roosevelt respected his guide for performing this unusual stunt and for another trick that he used to subdue rattlesnakes. The cowboy would corner a rattler and poke it until it coiled. Then, just as the snake was about to strike, he would take out his riding whip and snap off the rattler's head.

One day during a rabbit hunt the guide noticed

Roosevelt slip off his horse. Casually he rode over to Teddy to see if he needed any help. What he saw caused cold shivers to race down his back. The President stood, riding whip in hand, ready to strike a rattler over the head. Hurriedly the guide drew his gun and shot the snake. Later Roosevelt was soundly scolded for having broken his promise about taking unnecessary chances.

Although Roosevelt encountered many wild animals on his hunting excursions, he claimed that he had only one narrow escape. It was from a grizzly bear he had spotted on the opposite side of a thicket and wounded twice. The injured bear, filled with rage, charged through the brush. It came with such tremendous speed and at such an irregular gait that Teddy did not have time to raise his rifle and take careful aim. So he emptied both remaining barrels of the rifle magazine in the general direction of the charging beast. "After my last shot," recalled Roosevelt, "the first thing I saw was the bear's left paw as he struck at me, so close that I made a quick movement to one side. He was, however, practically already dead, and after another jump, and while in the very act of trying to turn to come at me, he collapsed like a shot rabbit."

Many wild animals lunged at Roosevelt while he was on his African safari, but the former Rough Rider shrugged off their attacks as routine experiences of the big-game hunter. Twice lions started to charge, but on both occasions he had enough time to fell them in their tracks.

Another time Roosevelt was reloading his gun when a bull elephant rushed him and came so near that it could have hit him with its trunk. But Teddy slipped behind a tree and calmly continued putting cartridges in his gun. Once Roosevelt diverted a rhinoceros while his hunting companions stalked buffalo. "That settles the question as to what we shall do with our ex-Presidents," he said. "They can be used to scare rhinos away."

Roosevelt's motive in going to Africa was not to see how many animals he could kill. Instead, he was commissioned by the Smithsonian Institution to collect big game, birds, reptiles, and plants. Whenever possible he wanted to bring back complete family groups of animals for museum display. From a scientific standpoint, his expedition was a great success. The former President returned home with hundreds of specimens of African life, including 296 pieces of game of seventy different species. In the animal collection were such rare items as hartebeests and bustards. After the trip Roosevelt concluded, "The mere size of bag indicates little as to man's prowess as a hunter and almost nothing as to the interest or value of the achievement."

Roosevelt always combined his hunting with his interest in natural science. John Burroughs, a fellow naturalist, pointed this out when he wrote, "I have never been disturbed by the President's hunting trips. It is to such men as he that the big game legitimately belongs — men who regard it from the point of view of the naturalist as well as from that of the sportsman, who are interested in its preservation . . ."

In 1887 Theodore Roosevelt conceived the idea of establishing a club of big-game hunters who were interested in encouraging sport with the rifle, promoting travel and exploration, and advocating the preservation of game. The organization was named the Boone and Crockett Club in honor of two pioneer hunters, and Roosevelt became its first president. Before long the Boone and Crockett Club was wielding considerable influence in promoting projects and legislation that would help curb the destruction of wildlife.

Theodore Roosevelt's cousin, Franklin, also combined the interests of the naturalist with the activities of the hunter. On his eleventh birthday he got his own gun, and he soon established a reputation among his playmates for being a fine shot. Young Franklin, who was fascinated by birds, decided he would start a home museum and include in his collection one of each species of bird that could be found in his part of the country. Soon he had scores of specimens, and they overflowed the shelves of the big mahogany cabinet in the library. All of the birds he had killed himself, and some of them he had even stuffed and mounted.

Another President who enjoyed hunting was Dwight Eisenhower. Nearly everyone who graduates from West Point learns to shoot well, and Eisenhower was no exception. On the way home from Korea in 1952 the President-elect shot down innumerable clay pigeons from the stern of a Navy cruiser. Occasionally Ike practiced his marksmanship on ducks, but his favorite game was quail. Several times while he was President he trekked to the plantation of Treasury Secretary George Humphrey in Thomasville, Georgia, to hunt quail.

For hours Eisenhower would tramp through the wet underbrush, plodding along until he had killed his limit of ten birds or the cover of darkness had driven him from the fields. But now and then the President and Secretary Humphrey abandoned the rugged tramping and hunted in the comfortable style of aristocratic Southern gentlemen. They rode in a carriage pulled by two white mules. A pair of pointers, trained to pick up the scent of the quail, bounded ahead of the carriage. When the dogs suddenly stopped and pointed in the direction of the birds, the President and his host climbed down from the carriage and readied their guns. Then a servant beat the underbrush with a leather strap. As the frightened birds scurried to get away and lifted their wings in flight, Eisenhower and Humphrey aimed and fired.

This was a far cry from the ways some other Presidents stalked their game. But hunting in comfort, while not very arduous, may have its merit, too. The quail, at any rate, taste much the same.

5

With Rod and Reel

Izaak Walton, the angling pioneer who wrote about his favorite sport in 1653, would have been proud of Herbert Hoover.

Before he became the thirty-first President of the United States, Hoover had been president of the Izaak Walton League of America. His inauguration speech to the fraternity of fishermen was laced with humor and so widely reprinted that it was estimated to have reached fifteen million persons. While he was the league president, he helped push through legislation and agreements to regulate fishing in American waters and stop pollution of streams.

Hoover frequently sang the praises of his favorite sport. In eloquent terms he once described fishing as "the chance to wash one's soul with pure air, with the rush of the brook, or with the shimmer of the sun on the blue water. It brings meekness and inspiration from the decency of nature, charity toward tackle-makers, patience toward fish, a mockery of profits and egos, a quieting of hate, a rejoicing that you do not have to decide a darned thing until next week. And it is disci-

pline in the equality of men — for all men are equal
before fish."

Most of our Presidents have shared Hoover's feelings
about the virtues of fishing, but Calvin Coolidge was,
for a while, an exception. In a 1925 press conference
Coolidge criticized fishing as a waste of time for anyone
but young boys and old men. The nation's fishermen
reacted to the President's innocent observation with bel-
lows that sounded as if they had simultaneously stepped
on fishhooks in their bare feet. Telegraph keys rattled
off angry protests to Washington, and chapters of the
Izaak Walton League passed scornful resolutions de-
nouncing Coolidge. But this was only the beginning of
the President's fishing troubles.

Perhaps to quiet the clamor of his critics, Coolidge
decided to try his hand at fishing in the summer of 1926.
He stayed at White Pine Camp, next to Lake Osgood
in the Adirondacks. His first catch was a four-pound
pike, which created such excitement that New York
Governor Al Smith had it stuffed. Mrs. Coolidge later
wrote that her husband did so well as an amateur angler
that the party had fresh fish on the table almost every
day.

The President's public relations suffered, however. He
posed for a photograph holding a pickerel he had sup-
posedly caught, and the picture was used in newspapers
throughout the country. But it failed to restore Coolidge's popularity with the fishing fanatics. News leaked

out that the tiny, hollow-eyed pickerel was dead before it had been put on the President's hook. Fisherman Coolidge was dressed for the picture in coat, tie, stiff collar, and a Panama hat too small for his head. He had an unhappy expression on his face and held the fish as far from his body as possible.

Coolidge had less trouble in the summer of 1928, when he vacationed at Cedar Island Lodge on a small island in Wisconsin's Brule River. Dressed in a red Mackinaw, high boots, ten-gallon hat, and khaki pants, he fished with a Chippewa Indian guide. The President carefully cast his line in a narrow river channel, which was rigged with concealed wire screens to keep the trout from escaping. The captive fish had been raised in a hatchery on a chopped liver diet, without Coolidge's knowledge. Although they had been too well fed to be very hungry, some of the trout eventually rose to the bait and ended up on the President's dinner table. When Coolidge took his first bite of the prize catch, he exclaimed in astonishment, "These damn fish taste like liver."

Reporters asked Coolidge how many fish were in the Brule, and he estimated forty-five thousand. "I haven't caught them all yet," he said, "but I've intimidated them." That summer the President invited Hoover, who was then the Republican candidate to succeed him in the White House, to visit his fishing camp. The two men spent several days together, casting for trout and talking politics. Coolidge would not tell reporters which man caught the most fish, but he did admit that "Mr.

Hoover is a better fisherman than I am."

Coolidge vacationed another time at the huge State Game Lodge in the Black Hills of South Dakota. There he fished in regal style. Attendants or Secret Service men put the bait on his hook and took off whatever fish were caught. Many big ones were hooked, partly because the President's fishing had improved and partly because the creek where he fished was blocked off and stocked with oversized trout.

All was going smoothly until a reporter, seeing Coolidge walk toward the lodge carrying five trout on a string, asked him if he had used a fly. Coolidge answered, "No, I used a hook and worm." To fly-fishermen, the Chief Executive might as well have admitted he beat his wife. "Worms!" screamed the New York *World*. "Words fail! Comment is useless! . . ." Even the politicians jumped on the unsuspecting President's use of worms. One irate senator cried, "There's no telling what a man will do who will catch trout with a worm." Another senator complained, "Any trout that would lie in bottom and bite at a worm is a degenerate trout." Some anglers came to the President's defense, and the controversy over flies versus worms raged in the nation's papers. Eventually the harassed Chief Executive switched to flies, but it is doubtful whether his conversion fully appeased the rabid fly-fishermen.

Hoover later commented on Coolidge's fishing troubles. "Whether President Coolidge fished in his youth is uncertain. He was a good deal of a fundamentalist in economics, government and fishing, so he naturally preferred angleworms. But when the fly-fishermen of the nation raised their eyebrows in surprise, he took to artificial flies. However, his back cast was so much a common danger that even the Secret Service men kept at a distance until they were summoned to climb trees to retrieve flies."

The subject of Coolidge's worm fishing came up unexpectedly on Hoover's 1937 fishing trip to the Northwest. The lady proprietor of a group of cabins near a roaring trout stream fixed breakfast for the President and O. Glenn Saxon of Yale University, who was vacationing with him. She was about to give Hoover some trout flies that she had tied herself when she suddenly stopped short. With a scornful expression, she said, "I hope that you don't use worms like President Coolidge." Hoover kept a straight face and answered, "No, I never stoop to such lowdown tactics, but this fellow Saxon here does — and don't give any of your flies to him — he wouldn't appreciate them."

Hoover was a confirmed fly-fisherman, but as a youth he, too, had started with worms and a butcher-string line. Once, on a boyhood fishing trip, Hoover and his chums were each given three artificial flies by a generous adult. The future President never had tried flies before, and he was delighted with the results they brought. He used his flies until all the feathers wore off, never dreaming that they were perishable.

To Hoover the rushing stream became a lifelong lure.

Even in his eighties he eagerly looked forward to those times when he could don old clothes, assemble his gear and tackle, and wade knee-deep in the icy water. Although he preferred fresh water angling, Hoover occasionally fished in the ocean. Once he made a battleship wait until he tried his luck in the Pacific. This happened late in 1928, when, as President-elect, he went on a goodwill cruise to Central and South America. Earlier that year he had tried in vain to get time off from his election campaign to fish. So when two little boats left the battleship near the tip of Lower California, Hoover boarded one of them and happily brought in a dolphin, weighing about ten pounds, and a mackerel.

Another President who shared Izaak Walton's enthusiasm for fishing was Grover Cleveland. Richard W. Gilder, editor of *Century Magazine* and the President's frequent fishing companion, said Cleveland ". . . will fish when it shines and fish when it rains; I have seen him pull bass up in a lively thunderstorm, and refuse to be driven from a Cape Cod pond by the worst hailstorm I ever witnessed or suffered. He will fish through hunger and heat, lightning and tempest . . . This, I have discovered, is the secret of 'Cleveland luck'; it is hard work and no let up."

Gilder said Cleveland was immoderate in only two things, desk work and fishing. The rotund Chief Executive usually was so interested in angling that he had to be reminded when it was time to eat. On Cape Cod one day his companions were unable to catch anything and went back to shore. But Cleveland stayed on, changing position and bait until he finally brought in a large bass. Proudly he showed his fish to his friends and displayed the fancy fly he had used to attract it. "I call this my restaurant fly," he said, "because the fish can get anything he likes on it."

As a boy in Fayetteville, New York, Cleveland developed the persistence that amazed his friends in later years. He was as curious as he was patient and once had his fingers bitten when trying to open the mouth of a huge muskellunge to see inside. When he was sheriff of Buffalo he and his friends often supplied the fish served at a local restaurant. He was serious about the sport and strict about its rules, always throwing back any fish below a certain size. A friend once hooked a big fish that was too heavy for him to bring in. When he asked for aid, Cleveland replied, "No, every fellow in this boat must pull in his own fish."

Like many other fishermen, Cleveland had his share of embarrassing moments. On one occasion the President and his physician, Dr. Joseph Bryant, decided to experiment with live frogs as bait to tempt the pickerel in a creek. Some little brown frogs were hooked through the skin of their backs and allowed to gyrate in the water to attract the attention of the fish. The doctor soon landed a good-sized pickerel, but Cleveland, impatiently puffing on a cigar, had no luck. Hours passed and Dr. Bryant's frogs kept attracting more and more pickerel, while Cleveland just sat and waited. Finally the President sighted a fine-looking frog across the creek on a stump and decided to substitute it for the one on his hook. He reeled in his line until it became taut. At the same time the frog on the stump curiously started to struggle. When Cleveland stopped reeling, the frog across the way relaxed. The frustrated fisherman realized that his wily frog had made its way over to the stump, hook and all, and rested in safety while the pickerel chased Dr. Bryant's bait. "I ought to have attended to business," said Cleveland and gave up fishing for the day.

A worthy member of the fishing fraternity was famous actor Joseph Jefferson, one of Cleveland's best friends. The President wrote to Jefferson: "Did it ever occur to you what a fortunate thing it is that you and I jointly are able to appreciate and enjoy a regular out-and-out outing, undisturbed by the question of fish captured? How many of our excursions have been thus redeemed! It really seems to be a kind of a low, sordid view to take of our excursions, to measure their success by the number of poor, slimy fish we are able to exhibit. Still we will not scorn them, and I have quite a lot of new-fangled gear for their capture."

Jefferson's last will and testament showed his deep affection for his fishing companion: "I bequeath to my friend, Honorable Grover Cleveland, my best Kentucky reel." It was this friendship that led Cleveland to buy Gray Gables, a summer house on Buzzards Bay in Massachusetts. The retreat was close to Jefferson's summer house, where Cleveland had spent enjoyable vacations. Gray Gables, when purchased between Cleveland's two stints in the White House, was accessible only by boat or a six-mile carriage drive.

The retreat was perfect for President Cleveland. Fishing for bass on the inland fresh-water ponds or for blue-fish on Buzzards Bay, he could forget the nation's troubles and patiently wait for a bite. Something about the atmosphere of the place seemed to keep his mind away from politics. One night Jefferson and some other friends gathered at Gray Gables to watch the returns from a national political convention come in over a private wire. At the peak of the excitement, Cleveland got up and walked out of the room, saying, "I do believe I forgot to dry my fishing line."

Benjamin Harrison, who occupied the White House between Cleveland's two terms, also found it beneficial to fish at a hideaway. His choice was Middle Bass Island in Lake Erie. He went there, despite a letter from a Kansas politician who warned, "For God's sake, Benjamin, do not get a fishing reputation at the start . . . take a fool's advice, and watch public opinion, and let Grover Cleveland go fishing."

Chester Arthur was a member of the Restigouche Salmon Fishing Club in Canada, where he once caught a record fifty-pound salmon. But he did not visit the club while President because he felt the Chief Executive should not leave the country. Still he managed to get in some fishing. In 1883 Arthur celebrated his fifty-second birthday while relaxing on a fishing jaunt to Alexandria Bay on the St. Lawrence River.

Another President who fished in a variety of locations was Dwight Eisenhower. He baited his hooks in such widely separated places as Maine, Mexico, South Dakota, Georgia, Wisconsin, and Colorado. During a vacation in the Maine wilderness in 1955 he stayed in a log cabin on Parmachenee Lake. But he did all his fishing in the nearby Magolloway River because the Secret Service men did not want him to go out on the lake in a canoe or small boat. This restriction proved to be a blessing in disguise, for Ike caught seventy trout in a single day.

Eisenhower was a fly-fisherman and often tied his own flies. He liked to devise impromptu lures on slow days when the fish were ignoring his line. "As for the dry fly," he said, "I just feel it's a more natural way to fish for trout." Flies led to trouble at an Eisenhower Cabinet meeting. Vice President Richard Nixon and Mrs. Oveta Culp Hobby, Secretary of Health, Education, and Welfare, gave the President a colorful assortment of flies on behalf of the Cabinet. Eisenhower could not resist a little practice with one of the flies. He made a gentle cast across the room and snared the seat of Press Secretary James Hagerty's trousers. The struggle to get the fly unhooked from Hagerty's pants proved as difficult as any problem discussed at the Cabinet meeting. Finally Eisenhower let his catch escape by cutting the fly away with a pocketknife.

Ike usually was a careful fisherman, rigging his own

rod and staying in the middle of the stream to cut down noise. He used an old-style bamboo pole and a hand-operated reel. "I used a bamboo rod when I started fishing as a kid," he said. "I just got used to it, that's all. I prefer the old-fashioned reel because I like to play my fish — wind the line myself . . ."

Ike tried to shrug off the gaping spectators who watched him on some of his fishing holidays. When he fished in the South Platte River in Colorado, crowds gathered on the highway above the river. Parents dragged along their children, cameras, and picnic baskets, and the spectacular view of the mountains was ignored as the curiosity seekers gawked at their President at play. Some shouted advice to the frustrated fisherman, and others called out messages of encouragement. Despite the noisy distractions, Ike held his temper and did his best to concentrate on rounding up trout.

In a spirit of Presidential togetherness, Eisenhower once invited former President Hoover to fish with him in Colorado. When the newspapermen swarmed about to catch a glimpse of the two famous men, Hoover appeared surprised. "I used to believe there were only two occasions in which the American people had regard for the privacy of the President — in prayer and in fishing," Hoover told Ike. "I now detect that you have lost the second part."

Hoover apparently had forgotten his own lack of privacy while he served as President. He had been frequently irritated by stories about his fishing trips get-

ting into the papers. When well-meaning officials started
to install a telephone in his California fishing camp, he
told them he had traveled thousands of miles to escape
from telephones. Hoover's main Presidential hideaway,
however, was much nearer Washington. This fishing
camp was built for him on the Rapidan River in the
Shenandoah National Park of Virginia. Every weekend
when he could escape from the capital, he took the three-
hour trip to his Rapidan retreat.

Franklin D. Roosevelt had a retreat in the Catoctin
Mountains of Maryland, but his happiest fishing experiences came on the ocean. Although he was unable to use
his polio-stricken legs for leverage, F. D. R.'s unusually
strong arm and shoulder muscles enabled him to be an
excellent deep-sea angler. Even after a long and tiring
day of battling big fish, he was likely to suggest, "We've
got another hour, so what about a bit of bottom fishing?"

He once told a press conference that his ocean cruises
were mainly to get a new perspective on Washington.
The piscatorial pursuits were just incidental, and "I don't
give a continental damn whether I catch a fish or not,"
he said. But when his son Elliott told reporters that
F. D. R. had had no luck one day off the Bahamas, the
President kiddingly accused the young man of "gross
libel" and rounded up witnesses to testify to his fishing
prowess.

All sorts of odd things from the ocean's depths were
hauled in by Roosevelt. In 1933, while cruising aboard
the gleaming white yacht, *Nourmahal,* he had absolutely

no luck with tuna and swordfish. But on the last day of the vacation he landed a 100-pound turtle. A scientist, Dr. Waldo Schmitt, went along on a 1938 cruise in which Roosevelt provided the Smithsonian Institution with some rare specimens that were later named in his honor. F. D. R. had a disagreement with Dr. Schmitt over the identification of one fish, and a check with an expert at the Smithsonian proved that Roosevelt was correct.

F. D. R. refused to cut his line whenever he hooked a shark, preferring instead to make a fight. On a 1940 cruise in the Pacific, he hauled in a 230-pound shark after an hour-and-a-half battle. Another time he caught a 250-pound shark after a fight that lasted almost three hours. He once hooked a sailfish off the Cocos Islands in the Pacific and was playing it when a second sailfish hit his line. The line formed a knot around the beak of the second fish. The first escaped, but sailfish number two was brought in. When Roosevelt had this fish displayed at the White House, the knot was still securely around its beak.

In 1941 Roosevelt informed the press he was going fishing off the Massachusetts island, Martha's Vineyard. Suspicions were aroused when he refused to take any reporters along. F. D. R. composed a daily message to the newspapermen, saying the weather was beautiful and the fishing good. Four days after leaving Washington, the Presidential yacht was joined in the foggy Atlantic by English ships. Roosevelt and Prime Minister

Winston Churchill met secretly at sea and drew up the historic Atlantic Charter.

Although not considered ardent fishermen, Harry Truman and John Kennedy did well on brief ocean outings. Truman, who had fished the Missouri and Little Blue rivers as a boy, had poor luck on an excursion to Puget Sound in 1945, but he made up for it the next year in the waters off Bermuda. Led by a guide and sporting a white pith helmet, Truman went out in a cabin cruiser and pulled in the biggest fish of the day, a 6½-pound dogfish. On his honeymoon to Acapulco in 1953, Kennedy caught a 99-pound sailfish, which measured nine feet, eight inches.

Our Presidents, from George Washington to Lyndon Johnson, have caught many different species of fish in places that are far apart. Johnson likes to angle for bass and catfish in the ponds and lakes of his native Texas. Washington usually fished in the Atlantic. On October 6, 1751, he caught a dolphin, a shark, and a pilot fish while on his way to Barbados in the West Indies. On the next day his diary said, ". . . a Dolphin we catchd. at Noon but cou'd not intice with a baited hook two Baricootas, wich played under our stern for some Hours; the Dolphin being small we had it dressed for Supper."

In 1789 Washington sailed outside the harbor of Portsmouth, Virginia. His diary reported, ". . . We proceeded to the Fishing Banks a little without the Harbour and fished for Cod; but it was not being a proper time of tide, we only caught two."

Washington fished for profit as well as pleasure, and the yield from the Potomac waters was second only to the yield from the Mount Vernon soil. He used seines to haul in great quantities of herring and shad. The surplus fish that were not needed to feed his own household were salted down in barrels and sold. In the single year of 1774 Washington's fishing business accounted for the sale of 905 barrels of herring.

The Father of Our Country liked fish on the table, as well as on the end of his line or in his nets. As a boy he helped reduce the fish populations of the Potomac and Rappahannock rivers. His diaries said he often "went a dragging for Sturgeon," and he hooked ". . . 2 Cat Fish of the size of our largest River Cats" on a 1770 expedition to the Ohio Valley. Three times between the sessions of the Constitutional Convention in 1787 Washington took his London-made rod and line and went fishing in the Philadelphia area.

Thomas Jefferson accompanied Washington in June of 1790 for a three-day fishing trip off Sandy Hook, New Jersey. A newspaper reported on the excursion: "Yesterday afternoon the President of the United States returned from Sandy Hook and the fishing banks, where he had been for the benefit of the sea air, and to amuse himself in the delightful recreation of fishing. We are told he has had excellent sport, having himself caught a great number of sea-bass and black fish. The weather proved remarkably fine, which, together with the salubrity of the air and wholesome exercise, rendered this little voyage extremely agreeable, and cannot fail, we hope, of being very serviceable to a speedy and complete restoration to health."

Some of our Presidents, however, were condemned by the press for taking time from their official duties for fishing trips. After he retired from public service, Grover Cleveland acknowledged that he had been a victim of such unpleasant publicity. But he brushed aside these attacks as "nothing more serious than gnat stings suffered on the bank of a stream." In fact, he felt rather sorry for the critics who did not share his devotion to fishing. "I sadly reflected," said Cleveland, "how their dispositions might have sweetened and their lives made happier if they had yielded something to the particular type of frivolity which they deplored."

Izaak Walton could not have said it any better.

6

On the Links

Woodrow Wilson toured the golf courses in and around Washington more often than any other President. Making his rounds as faithfully as a postman, he refused to let anything interfere with his exercise and enjoyment of the outdoors. The President played late in the afternoon or at five in the morning, whenever the mood struck him. It was common for members of the White House staff to see him leave for a golfing excursion before dawn bundled in a warm sweater and cap. He once burned a hand on an exhaust pipe while inspecting a tank but was out on the links one week later swinging one-handed. Even snow could not stop him if he felt like golfing. He simply had the balls painted red so they could be easily seen on the white ground.

It mattered little to Wilson if his score was 90 or 190. In a sport notorious for causing short tempers, he seemed to enjoy just batting the ball around the fairways, regardless where it landed. The President never worried about mastering the finer points of the game. This carefree attitude was reflected in his humorous description of golf as "an ineffectual attempt to put an elusive ball into an obscure hole with an implement ill-adapted to the purpose."

Dr. Cary T. Grayson, Wilson's physician, encouraged the Chief Executive to golf often and also served as his most frequent companion on the links. The two of them, equally poor at the game, played almost every day. Dr. Grayson later recalled that Wilson was criticized for having so few golfing companions. "But," the doctor explained, "he found that most men whom he invited to play with him insisted on introducing public business into the conversation."

The President wanted no part of politics while he was golfing. He needed these periods of relaxation to take his mind off his heavy duties. A quiet round of golf could work wonders with his disposition. He could arrive at the course in a grumpy mood and leave a few hours later light-hearted and refreshed.

Wilson, however, would tolerate no distractions while he played. One afternoon he was strolling down a fairway when a boy on the edge of the course cupped his hands and made repeated Indian calls. "That boy must be training to be a senator," Wilson snapped. "He is always making a noise with his mouth and not saying anything."

Wilson played so frequently during his public career that he often received important messages while lining up shots. He had just made a good approach shot one day when a messenger ran up and informed him that he had been nominated as the Democratic candidate for governor of New Jersey. Wilson listened to the exciting news and then calmly sank his putt. When he was President, Wilson received on the golf course the shocking report that the *Lusitania* had been sunk in the Atlantic. He also played golf on the fateful day that Nikolai Lenin became premier of Russia. On another occasion he was reminded to hustle through his game in order to attend a White House tea. At this tea Wilson met Mrs. Edith Bolling Galt, who later became his second wife.

The first Mrs. Wilson died seventeen months after her husband's inauguration, and the President started golfing more than ever to occupy his hours of loneliness. After a while he began seeing Mrs. Galt, who he discovered liked golf too. Part of their courtship took place on the links, with Secret Service men acting as chaperons. They also went golfing on their honeymoon at Hot Springs, Virginia, and continued playing regularly after they returned to Washington. The newlyweds golfed almost every morning, and even though Mrs. Wilson needed 200 strokes to finish the course, neither she nor her husband showed the slightest concern over their scores.

Wilson's successor in the White House, Warren Harding, also was a frequent golfer. As in Wilson's case, Harding's doctors heartily approved his playing. But unlike his predecessor, Harding had a genuine interest in his score and worked hard to improve his strokes. A senator who golfed with Harding said of him, "For the length of time he has played, less than three years, he plays a remarkably good game, and he gets the keenest kind of enjoyment out of it. His game is steadily improving, and he will become an exceptionally good player if he gives the time and practice necessary for one to become proficient in the game." Harding's secretary confided to friends that the President was "tickled to death" if he shot in the low 90's. He usually toured the Chevy Chase Club course in 95 and often finished in the 80's on other courses.

Although Harding laughed and joked with his golfing companions, and occasionally took along his dog, Laddie Boy, he still managed to concentrate on his game. During his first round after receiving the nomination to run for President, he was constantly followed by photographers. Nevertheless, he refused to be distracted and made good scores of 5, 5, 5, 3, and 5 for the first five holes. Another time Harding was playing before a large group of motion picture cameramen and five hundred spectators. The others in the foursome were nervous and either sliced or topped their drives, but Harding nonchalantly stepped up to the tee and belted a 200-yard drive. When asked how he did so well while surrounded by grinding cameras, he said, "Why, I think only of driving straight, look at the ball, and hit it easily." However, noisy cameras did cause him to look up while putting in a Newspaper Golf Association tournament in Washington. He missed his putt, and it cost him first place in the match.

Harding used a three-quarter swing on his drives,

sacrificing distance for control and accuracy. Even so, he often managed to get off drives of more than two hundred yards. His best shots were pitches to the green, and his putting, with a center-shafted stick, was reasonably good. Harding generally did better on the last nine holes and much preferred a one-stroke victory to an easy win.

The President's gambling spirit was aroused by water hazards, and he used a short mashie niblick to get over them. Sportswriter Grantland Rice described how Harding handled a sixty-yard pitch to the green over a stream. "The ball was lying badly in a patch bereft of all grass . . ." said Rice. "Yet he went after the short, high pitch without a quiver, dropped the ball eight feet from the cup, and sank his putt for a par three." Rice said the President had a strong, firm touch on putts but had the common fault of starting his body ahead of his hands.

Harding always stuck closely to the rules. He never moved his ball when it was in a bad spot, and he tried to avoid receiving special treatment. When a young man ran up to him on the fairway one day and handed him a rubber tee that he had forgotten, Harding remarked to his companion, "I wish the folks would forget once in a while that I am President." On another occasion friends told him to go ahead and pick up a bad lie. But Harding said, "Forget that I am President of the United States. I'm Warren Harding, playing with some friends, and I'm going to beat the hell out of them."

Playing with Harding could be a trying experience. When a rain started one afternoon, the President told his companions, "If you boys don't mind this, I don't." The others bravely agreed to go ahead with the game and teed off from the slippery turf. By the end of the game Harding was drenched from head to foot. Still he enjoyed the outing and was especially happy about a clean shot he made from a rain-filled ditch.

Harding had a habit of walking down the fairways at such a clip that it was hard for his companions to keep up. This got him in trouble one time at the Burning Tree Country Club. Harding teed off and walked ahead along the edge of the fairway. Next up was Ring Lardner, the famous humorist. Lardner sliced the ball, and it struck a tree branch above Harding. The branch fell down and hit the Chief Executive on the shoulder. Lardner was not at all concerned that he had startled the President of the United States. He casually strolled over to Harding and said, "I did all I could to make Coolidge President." Harding laughed so hard he dropped his club.

By playing golf, Harding lent the prestige of the Presidency to the game. He served as a member of the U.S. Golf Association and donated the President Warren Harding Cup for the National Public Links Championship. But after Harding died, White House closets contained few golf clubs until Dwight Eisenhower's administration.

Calvin Coolidge golfed even less than he talked. "I

have played the game only a little," he said in 1926. "I think it is a fine method of relaxation for men in business life, but like everything else which is an outside enterprise, it can undoubtedly be carried to excess." Another time he complained, "You have to dress for golf . . . Then you have to drive out to some club . . . It takes three hours to play a round, then you have to undress, take a shower, dress again, and drive back . . . Callers at the White House might wonder why the President wasn't on the job."

Because of his built-in New England thrift, Silent Cal rebelled against the cost of the game the few times he played. When golfing with professional Freddie McLeod, Coolidge swung, missed the ball, and accidentally broke his club on the ground. He anxiously turned to McLeod and said, "Freddie, that can be fixed, can't it?"

Herbert Hoover was not interested in golf, but Franklin D. Roosevelt probably would have been one of the White House's finest players if he had not been stricken by polio. He played well as a student at Harvard and continued the game until his illness. During the period when he was Assistant Secretary of the Navy, F. D. R. scored in the high 80's and enjoyed playing with a Republican senator by the name of Warren Harding. Burning Tree Country Club still has one of his brassies on display, along with the clubs of several other Presidents.

F. D. R. learned the game by accident. Once when he was sailing near his summer home at Campobello Island, a dense fog settled and forced him to drop anchor at a nearby port and stay with friends. He learned to golf during the visit and came home to Campobello determined to take up the game in earnest. With characteristic enthusiasm, he built a makeshift course on his vacation island and launched a tournament. It was one of the most unusual tournaments ever held, for the sheep that grazed on Campobello constituted the major hazards. "And as no call of 'fore' penetrated their wooly skulls," wrote Roosevelt's mother, "the players simply had to aim well over the cropping heads, shut their eyes, and hope for the best. Franklin won the championship, but it is difficult now to remember whether the score was recorded in strokes or sheep."

Outspoken Harry Truman, who caused a controversy when he wrote a blistering letter to a critic who had scorned his daughter's singing, once found it necessary to write a letter defending himself against a false accusation concerning golf. "For your information," asserted Truman, "I never played golf in my life, never had a golf club in my hands to tell the honest truth, except to look at it — so I couldn't possibly have fired a ball on the Independence (Missouri) golf course and hit anybody on the head."

Unlike Truman, Lyndon Johnson has had a golf club in his hands, and he plays the game occasionally. But he does not find it particularly enjoyable, and he refuses to take the time to practice his strokes. Usually Johnson carries on a business conversation while playing golf. When he was a senator he would now and then visit

Burning Tree Country Club and leisurely cover the course while discussing ideas with other government officials.

Dwight Eisenhower probably did more for golf than any other Chief Executive. "People like to follow the leader," observed the operator of Washington's public golf courses shortly after General Ike became President. "The papers keep talking golf. People start talking golf and then start playing it. I tell you, the President really has given the game a shot in the arm . . . Ever since he went into the White House, all you hear is golf, golf, golf."

The game in turn was good for Eisenhower. His physician, Major General Howard Snyder, said, "Golf is a tonic for the President. It is good for his nerves and his muscle tone, and it takes his mind off the scores of anxieties that confront him daily." When some critics claimed Eisenhower spent too much time on the links, Snyder stoutly defended the President's frequent golf excursions. "Golf is fine for him," he insisted, "so I say he should play whenever he gets a chance. He doesn't get away from the office nearly as much as I'd like him to do." Eisenhower agreed with his doctor's advice. He told a press conference in 1958 that his three outdoor hobbies, golf, fishing, and shooting, were beneficial and chained his mind to ball, trout, or bird — and nothing else.

Although he first played golf in 1927, Eisenhower did not take up the game seriously until after the Second

World War. When he did become an avid golfer he worked hard to better his play. He took lessons. He practiced diligently. He rejoiced over good shots and felt discouraged when his game was not going well.

The names of courses that Eisenhower regularly played became familiar to millions of Americans who never in their lives went golfing. High on his list of favorite courses was the Augusta National Golf Club at Augusta, Georgia. The site each year of the famous Masters Tournament, Augusta was frequented by professionals and important businessmen, the President's favorite partners. Ike tried to arrange his schedule to visit Augusta several times a year. He particularly liked to go there shortly after the Masters to play with some of the professional stars and have the tournament described by friends. While chatting with his golf cronies, he often wore his emerald green Augusta National Golf Club blazer with the club emblem. The club members built a large, elegant "cabin" for their distinguished visitor and his wife, Mamie, in a grove of pine trees not far from the tenth hole.

In the capital the President generally played Wednesdays and Saturdays at Burning Tree. As a member of the club, he once was invited to compete in the District of Columbia Senior Golf Championship for golfers fifty-five or older. He declined, saying, "Maybe someday when I'm eligible in the 90-year class."

The most unusual playing site for Eisenhower was at Camp David, the Presidential hideaway in the Catoctin

Mountains of Maryland. Designed by an Augusta friend, the pitch-and-putt course at Camp David had only one green but four approaches, each at a different distance and level. The course was installed in a clearing below the rustic lodge where the President and his family lived.

Ed Dudley, the pro at Augusta, helped Eisenhower improve his game. When Dudley first observed his play, Ike had a bad habit of trying to kill the ball off the tee, with all his power coming from the right hand and arm. His trick knee would pop out if he twisted his leg too sharply. To protect the knee he was overcompensating and slicing most of his drives. Dudley patiently worked with his pupil to gain control of his slice and get his left hand and arm into the swing.

"The President shoots a lot better golf than I thought he would," said Cary Middlecoff, another pro. "The main trouble with his game is that he doesn't have an opportunity to play enough." Middlecoff felt that Ike's drives and middle shots were very good. "He can belt one 225 yards off the tee and knock it a pretty good chunk from the fairway," the pro commented. "Ike is a little weak from 75 to 100 yards out, but that can be attributed to his lack of play. He chips exceptionally well," Middlecoff added.

Eisenhower usually shot in the middle 80's, but at times he could not crack 90. A 95 would make him irritable and angry with himself, and a score in the high 80's would never satisfy him. But Ike was pleased when he could complete a round in the middle or low 80's. In

1954 he shot a five-over-par 77 at the Cherry Hills Country Club near Denver. He broke 80 various times at Burning Tree, Augusta, and Gettysburg. After he stepped down from the Presidency, Eisenhower went to Palm Desert, California, for winter golfing vacations. There he often shot in the low 80's.

Football coach Frank Leahy described golfer Eisenhower as "quite a competitor . . . he never gives up." Reporters assigned to cover the President said that if Eisenhower had the time he would stay on the course and practice a muffed shot until he had it right. But after his heart attack in 1955, Ike was warned by his doctors not to play so intently. In one of his first rounds following his illness, Ike told his partners, "You're going to hear a heck of a lot of laughter today. My doctor has given me orders that if I don't start laughing instead of cussing when I miss those shots, he's going to stop me from playing golf. So every time I miss a shot you're going to hear a haw-haw-haw." In 1956 Eisenhower won the Ben Hogan Trophy for being the player whose recovery from a physical ailment most inspired the community of golfers.

The nationwide interest in Eisenhower's golfing was heightened when, early in 1953, he went out to the south lawn of the White House and practiced chipping balls to an imaginary green. His valet shagged the balls for him. Soon newsmen and spectators gathered at the fence, and some motorists even left their cars in the street to run up and take a look. Before long, the practice session had caused a traffic jam, and the disgruntled golfer was forced to retreat to his office.

After this unfortunate experience, the President had to develop a special routine for practicing shots in his own backyard. Whenever a crowd assembled at the fence, he would duck into a police shack on the White House grounds and wait until the spectators went away. Usually he would have to repeat this procedure two or three times, and even then some hangers-on might linger to catch a glimpse of the President at play. Ike resented the commotion that was caused whenever he played on his own lawn. "You know," he remarked, "once in a while I get to the point, with everybody staring at me, where I want to go way back indoors and pull down the curtain."

In 1954 the U.S. Golf Association had a putting green installed in the more private area just outside Ike's office. It had a small sand trap on one side and two undersized holes to sharpen his putting. White House gardeners had to repair the divots in the lawn after Ike took his chipping practice. One friend suggested to the President that he would be a good target for an assassin while golfing on the lawn. But Ike just grinned and replied, "Point out one of those fellers to me and I'll show you a direct hit at 250 yards."

Eisenhower was not the only President to use the White House grass for golf practice. Warren Harding recognized the possibility of turning the south lawn into a fairway. He teed off from an old carpet spread over the turf, and his dog, Laddie Boy, did most of the retrieving. John Kennedy also took advantage of the spacious south lawn. He placed a door mat on the grass and practiced chip shots off it with seven-, eight-, and nine-irons.

Until his back started bothering him, the athletic Mr. Kennedy was the best, if not the most ardent, White House golfer. The youngest man ever elected to the highest office in the land played for a while on the freshman golf team at Harvard. Then he consistently shot in the 70's, and after college days he generally finished in the 80's. Fred Corcoran of the Professional Golfers Association compared Kennedy as a golfer to the other Presidents who played the game: "If there were a match among the five Presidents who played golf, Kennedy would win, Eisenhower would finish second about four strokes behind him, and Wilson, Harding, and Taft would all have trouble breaking 100. Kennedy can hit a tee shot as far as 250 yards even though he prefers a spoon (number three wood) to a driver."

But Kennedy refused to concentrate intently on the game. "Jack never fusses," said Bert Nicolls, a pro at Palm Beach, Florida. "He just walks up and hits the ball." Once Kennedy teed off in his usual brisk fashion, and the drive went awry. Bouncing off a palm tree, the ball hit a Secret Service man on the head. The President insisted that he see a doctor immediately, but the embarrassed guard was not seriously injured.

The Secret Service men have had their troubles while

guarding the golfing Presidents. In addition to the constant danger of getting hit by a stray shot, they had to caddy occasionally for Wilson and Harding, trail along while Wilson courted his second wife, help Harding keep track of his bets, and wear inconspicuous sports shirts to please Eisenhower. In earlier days only one or two Secret Service men accompanied the Presidents at play. But during the Eisenhower and Kennedy administrations agents tramped along both sides of the fairways with shortwave radios and carbines concealed in their golf bags.

The public has been more critical of golf than any other sport the Presidents have played. "It would seem incredible that anyone would care one way or the other about your playing golf, but I have received literally hundreds of letters from the West protesting about it . . ." wrote Theodore Roosevelt to William Howard Taft during the Presidential campaign of 1908. Roosevelt, who had tried golf and found it "undemocratic" and "too much of a sissy game," sent an additional note of warning to the man he hoped would succeed him in the White House: "I myself play tennis, but that game is a little more familiar; besides, you never saw a photograph of me playing tennis. I'm careful about that; photographs on horseback, yes; tennis, no. And golf is fatal."

In a campaign speech at Wolsey, South Dakota, Taft defended his favorite sport. "They said that I have been playing golf this summer," he told his audience, "and that it was a rich man's game, and that it indicated I was out of sympathy with the plain people. I want to state my case before the bar of public opinion on the subject of that game of golf . . . It is a game for people who are not active enough for baseball or tennis, or who have too much weight to carry around to play those games; and yet when a man weighs 295 pounds you have to give him some opportunity to make his legs and muscles move, and golf offers that opportunity." Paying little attention to Teddy, Taft made no secret of his love of the links and won the Presidency anyway.

After Taft won the election, he continued to golf two or three times a week. In spite of his weight, he was a fairly good player, although his form was most peculiar. He used a baseball grip, and his huge girth forced his swing to be short and choppy. His scores were most often in the 90's, but sometimes he finished in the 80's, which was quite respectable for a man his size who never took a lesson.

Taft joked about his own game, labeling it "bumble-puppy" golf. But he praised the sport as healthful recreation. "So invigorating is the air, you simply cannot loaf," he once wrote. "You just have to go out and bang the little white ball around. Then, when you have taken so much exercise, you sleep well at night, and when you sleep well, you are ready for another round the next day."

Taft was not the first Presidential golfer, nor the first to be criticized for playing the game. William McKinley golfed at Hot Springs, Virginia, in 1899. Describing the event, a newspaper in proper Boston reported that some citizens had objected because the President allowed spectators to watch him play. But the question of whether he should play in public never became a serious problem, since McKinley was not enthusiastic about golf. In the summer of 1897, when golf was a new sport in the United States, McKinley spent part of the summer at a resort near a golf course. Halfheartedly he tried the game but after a few holes gave it up in favor of reading in the shade of a favorite tree.

Harding was very sensitive to charges that he golfed too much. He once promised to see a Will Rogers stage performance, but changed his mind when he heard about the cowboy humorist's satirical description of the President talking golf throughout a Cabinet meeting. Four decades later another golfing politician faced an even more delicate situation. When Kennedy was campaigning for the Presidency in 1960, he was aware of the attacks that had been leveled at Eisenhower for his many golf sessions. So the Democratic candidate did not permit anyone to photograph him on a golf course until after the votes had been counted.

A 1953 Gallup Poll showed that less than 17 percent of the public felt Eisenhower took too much time for the game. The criticism of Ike's golf often took the form of good-natured jokes and wisecracks. His White House staff denied one story that he swung a golf club in his office while dictating letters to his secretary. A gag making the rounds had Ike and his companions asking to play through a slow foursome in front of them because New York had just been bombed. An automobile bumper sticker proclaimed, "Ben Hogan for President. If we're going to have a golfer, let's have a good one." Topping them all, one jokester observed, "I suppose that we'll have a national holiday if he ever makes a hole in one."

7

In the Saddle

IF anyone had tried to convince Theodore Roosevelt that riding was a genteel sport, he would have been in for a strenuous argument.

As a young man Roosevelt liked to ride to the hounds near his home on Long Island. One bright morning he set out with some companions on an invigorating chase. All went well until the riders approached a five-foot wall. Roosevelt's horse leaped high, but struck the top rail and rolled over on its side on a pile of stones. Teddy staggered to his feet, with his face dripping blood from several deep gashes. Wiping his face with his handkerchief, he climbed back in the stirrups and, by hard riding, managed to be in at the death of the fox.

Returning from the chase, Roosevelt was in high spirits. No one suspected that the hardy hunter had suffered anything worse than a badly scratched face. He never mentioned it to his companions, but Teddy had broken his arm in the fall. Describing the incident in a letter to Henry Cabot Lodge, he wrote: "I rode straight through the rest of the hunt. . . . I don't grudge the broken arm a bit. . . . I am always willing to pay the piper when I have had a good dance; and every now and then I like to drink the wine of life with brandy in it."

Roosevelt took some other bad spills when he was ranching in the West. In those days he was in the saddle for very long stretches — once for forty straight hours and another time for twenty-four hours. Cowboy Teddy rode the range, herded wild horses, lassoed stubborn steers, and tried to tame bucking broncos. After one fall from a bronco he emerged with a cracked rib, and a later fall resulted in a broken shoulder point. Both injuries were extremely painful, but Teddy was hundreds of miles from a doctor. So he simply gritted his teeth and went on working as usual, until the injuries finally healed themselves.

After he moved to the White House, Roosevelt continued to ride hard and often. He thoroughly enjoyed brisk gallops on bitterly cold days when the Washington bridle paths were covered with snow and ice. And in the sweltering summertime he took great delight in cantering far ahead of the perspiring Secret Service guards, who were nearly overcome by the heat. Another of his favorite equestrian pastimes was jumping. On Bleistein, his large, strong bay, Teddy sailed over tall fences and cleared bars as high as five feet eight inches.

Once, when he was not astride Bleistein, Roosevelt was riding in the company of a Cabinet member. The other man jumped his horse over a stone wall and a hurdle. Unable to resist a dare, rambunctious Teddy urged his reluctant mount to jump the same obstacles. The nervous horse cleared them with only inches to spare. "I could not let one of my Cabinet give me a lead and not follow," remarked the satisfied President.

Probably Roosevelt's most notable ride was when he led the famous Seventh Cavalry over Chickamauga battlefield in the first year of his Presidency. Mounting a spirited Army horse at the entrance to the memorial park, the President led the way into the reservation. As the riders fell in behind in squadron formation, Roosevelt asked the colonel to give the order "Forward, trot!" Soon the trot developed into a gallop, and the President's steed shot forward with the whole cavalcade thundering at his heels. A patch of pine trees loomed ahead, but the riders continued at full speed. Through the maze of trees and tangled underbrush for a mile and a half the company zigzagged. During the mad chase about a dozen men were thrown from their horses, and the ambulance corps had to pick up the lame, the halt, and the badly bumped. But the President, who had come through the ordeal without even a scratch, was delighted and made a brief speech complimenting the men on their excellent riding.

Roosevelt's daring feats on horseback gave government officials cause for concern. "The President came in this morning badly bunged up about the head and face," wrote Secretary of State John Hay in his diary on October 23, 1904. "His horse fell with him yesterday and gave him a bad fall. It did not occur to me until after he had gone that I had come so near a fatal elevation to a short term of the Presidency." Less than two weeks later Hay recorded an even more sober note in his diary. "The President's fall from his horse, ten days ago, might have been very serious. He landed fairly on his head, and his neck and shoulders were severely wrenched. For a few days there seemed to be a possibility of meningitis." Then he added a prophetic reflection about the strenuous Chief Executive. "The President will, of course, outlive me, but he will not live to be old."

Other Presidents, besides Roosevelt, had some serious riding mishaps. Shortly after Thomas Jefferson resigned as governor of Virginia, he took his favorite horse on a fast gallop. The mount slipped and Jefferson fell, breaking an arm and collarbone. Another time, when he was an old man in retirement, Jefferson was astride a horse that slipped while fording a river, and he became entangled in the reins and almost drowned. A few years later James Monroe fractured a wrist in a fall from a horse. Much more dangerous was the accident that befell Abraham Lincoln when, as a boy, he was driving a horse at a mill. The horse, hitched to a beam, was slowly following a circular path and providing the power to grind the grain. Impatient young Abe was urging the beast on with a few strokes of the switch when suddenly the horse let loose with a swift kick which sent the boy sprawling to the ground. Bleeding and motionless, he was carried home, where he lay in a coma until the next morning.

Several future Presidents had close calls while riding horses in the thick of battle. Franklin Pierce was seriously injured in the Mexican War when his horse, frightened by the crack of a rifle, reared and tossed him on a jagged lava rock. During the Civil War four horses were killed under Rutherford B. Hayes. Once when this happened Hayes was hurled violently to the ground and knocked unconscious. In the same war both James A. Garfield and Ulysses S. Grant were fortunate to escape unharmed when their horses were hit by bullets. But Grant was not so lucky on another occasion. He raced his horse against the mount of a young Kentucky officer, and the two riders dashed along neck and neck until they came to a bend in the road that revealed an approaching train. Suddenly Grant's horse swerved from its course, and the general plunged over its head. Grant sustained an injury which left him crippled for several weeks.

In April 1862, during the bloody Battle of Shiloh, Grant had to advance under the cover of nightfall. Crossing over a heavy log in the darkness, his horse slipped and fell on Grant's leg. The general's ankle became swollen, and for several days he had to use crutches. Harry Truman was another President who had a horse fall on him. This occurred during the First World War while Truman was fighting in France. In the midst of a barrage from German guns, his horse fell in a shell hole and rolled on him. Scampering unhurt to his feet, he barely escaped the enemy fire. Another time, while directing a night attack, Truman cantered his horse past low-hanging branches which swept his

West Pointer Dwight D. Eisenhower takes a practice kick.

Worn knees show that John F. Kennedy and his teammates took their football seriously at Dexter School.

Photo by Ollie Atkins, The Saturday Evening Post

Senator John F. Kennedy tosses the ball to his brother Robert in a friendly game of touch football.

The Abilene, Kansas, baseball team of 1909, with Dwight D. Eisenhower sitting front and center.

Wide World Photos

William Howard Taft opens the 1911 baseball season.

John F. Kennedy doing the same, in 1961, with fan, Lyndon B. Johnson looking on.

A collegiate pugilist, Theodore Roosevelt.

Out duck hunting, Grover Cleveland takes aim from his rowboat.

Big game. Theodore Roosevelt poses with a rhinoceros he has just felled.

Dwight D. Eisenhower waits in the surrey that will take him to the quail.

No fisherman himself, Calvin Coolidge seems to show his distaste when photographed with a fish.

Angler Herbert Hoover tries his luck in the Housatonic.

Harry S. Truman stands proudly between two naval men who help him display his Bermuda catch.

Presidential golfer William Howard Taft with his putter.

Brown Brothers

Underwood and Underwood

Woodrow Wilson lining up the ball in Princeton, New Jersey, in 1910.

Warren G. Harding seems to have hit a long one while spectators look on in 1923.

The end of a swing. Dwight D. Eisenhower at one of his favorite sports.

Theodore Roosevelt takes his horse, Bleistein, over a rail fence.

Lyndon B. Johnson and his first press secretary on horseback at the LBJ ranch.

Franklin D. Roosevelt catches up on the news beside the Warm Springs Foundation pool.

A member of the Harvard swimming team, John F. Kennedy prepares to dive.

Wide World Photos

kipper Franklin D. Roosevelt at the wheel of the *Half Moon* off Campobello, bout 1904.

John F. Kennedy emerges from the surf to the waiting arms of California fans

Helmsman, John F. Kennedy, chats with shipmates in Boothbay Harbor.

glasses from his face. Nearly frantic because his vision had been impaired at such a crucial time, he turned about in desperation. Good fortune was with him, for the moonlight revealed his glasses lying on the horse's back just behind the saddle.

In spite of the numerous accidents that plagued them during hazardous rides, many of our Presidents were expert horsemen. Probably no other Chief Executive spent as much time in the saddle as did George Washington, and Jefferson described him as "the best horseman of the age and the most graceful." Washington's horses traveled long distances, trod dangerous paths on surveying expeditions, charged into battle in two wars, galloped across the woods on fox hunts, pranced at the head of colorful parades, and cantered over the broad fields of the Mount Vernon plantation. "Those who have seen Washington on horseback," observed his adopted grandson George Washington Parke Custis, "will admit that he was one of the most accomplished of cavaliers in the true sense and perfection of the character. He rode, as he did everything else, with ease, with elegance, and with power."

While he was still in his teens, Washington earned the reputation of being a splendid rider. According to a story told by Custis, the youthful Virginian once tried to break an especially fierce colt that belonged to his mother. Others had tried to mount this ill-tempered sorrel, but it always reared with such fury and viciousness that each attempt had failed. The colt remained unbroken, roaming the fields and woods at will, tossing its mane to the wind, and defying any rider to approach. It was commonly said that a man never would be found who was strong enough to stay astride the savage animal.

Washington was determined to tame his mother's ungovernable colt. He told the other neighborhood boys that if they would help him hold the colt so that a bridle bit could be forced in its mouth, he would try to ride it. The boys agreed to help, and early one morning they chased the colt into a fenced enclosure and tied it with a rope. Then they forced its mouth open and pushed a bit inside. Springing upon the colt's back, Washington ordered the boys to untie the rope. With a sudden spurt the furious sorrel leaped to its freedom and raced for the open fields.

Wildly the colt reared and plunged, trying desperately to unseat the young rider. Washington's companions, breathlessly watching the terrific struggle between horse and boy, trembled for fear they had launched their friend on a fatal mission. But the youth stuck firmly on the horse's bare back, holding tightly to the reins with his powerful hands. Gathering all its strength for one mighty effort, the enraged colt reared high in the air with tremendous violence. Then suddenly it fell to the ground, with blood gushing from its nostrils. Washington, unharmed, climbed off the horse's back. Sadly he looked at the dead colt that had burst a blood vessel in its furious effort to keep from being tamed.

The Father of Our Country preferred to ride fleet-footed horses. He once said, "I require but one good quality in a horse — to go along." Of his numerous war horses his favorite was Nelson, a large swift sorrel with white legs and head. In many battles Nelson was the general's mount, and this calm, steady stallion could always be counted on to remain unruffled in the face of heavy fire and great excitement. The charger most frequently ridden by Washington after he became President was Prescott, a pure white parade horse that stood sixteen hands high. Prescott was indifferent to the noise of artillery and the waving of banners, but the stallion had a bad habit of dancing about whenever a carriage approached. This was annoying to the Chief Executive, who desired to ride as quietly as possible. Prescott's antics were especially embarrassing on the Saturday rides when Washington frequently met carriages carrying ladies who wanted to stop and pay their respects to the President.

The noted writer Washington Irving said of the first President, "If there was anything he was likely to take a pride in, it was horses; he was passionately fond of that noble animal." At one time he had as many as one hundred and forty horses at Mount Vernon, and his stables were widely known for their excellent quality. Washington was a skilled judge of horseflesh, and he prided himself on making expert purchases and trades. Once he was considering a pair of gray horses, and to be sure of what he was getting he paid the seller's coachman five shillings to tell him what he honestly thought about the animals. But occasionally his horse deals may have caused some embarrassment, such as the time when he was brought before a justice of the peace and fined for trading horses on Sunday.

The grooming of President Washington's saddle horses was performed with the greatest care. The night before they were to be ridden, the animals were covered with a whitish paste, swathed in body cloths, and left to sleep upon clean straw. By morning the paste had hardened and was well rubbed in before the grooms curried and brushed the horses' coats. This process gave their coats a glossy satinlike appearance. Then the hoofs were blackened and polished, the mouths were washed, and the teeth were picked and cleaned. Leopard skins were placed on the animals' backs, but only after the head groom had passed a fresh handkerchief over the flanks to make sure they were ready for the finest of horsemen.

Horses were always of great interest to Washington, even during the busiest times in his career. Gilbert Stuart, the famous artist who painted his portrait, said, "I found that it was difficult to interest him in conversation while I was taking his portrait. I began on the Revolution — the battles of Monmouth and Princeton, but he was absolutely dumb. After a while I got on horses. Then I touched the right chord."

Grant was another President who liked to talk about horses. He told a friend it was better to choose your own hobby than to have one pinned on you by the newspapers. So he had selected horses, and when anyone

tried to bring up an embarrassing topic, he would "turn
the conversation on the horse." It was said that politicians used to come away from the White House com-
plaining that they could not get any information from
Grant. "When I talk politics he talks horses," grunted
one frustrated politico.

From early childhood Grant had a keen knowledge of
horses. While still a toddler he liked to play in the barn
and swing himself on the farm horses' tails. One morning a neighbor saw him swinging in this hazardous manner and rushed to tell his mother that her little tike was
in momentary danger of being kicked to pieces. Mrs.
Grant received the announcement with complete calm,
assuring the horrified neighbor that her son understood
horses and they understood him.

Grant was not yet nine when he began the man-sized
chore of handling a team in the field. This was hard
work, but it was the kind of experience he enjoyed.
Everything that involved horsemanship intrigued the
boy, and there was no phase of this complicated subject
that escaped his attention. Word of his exceptional skill
with horses spread. Soon the neighboring farmers began
calling on him to teach their horses to pace or to break
their ill-tempered colts. And the pudgy young Ulysses
always proved equal to the difficult task.

Once a circus came to town with a trick pony, and
during the performance a clown offered five dollars to
any boy who could ride the lively animal. Many boys
tried, but the pony always dumped them unceremoni-

ously to the ground. Finally, when it appeared that no one could master the tricky little beast, Ulysses stepped forward and climbed on its back. Round and round the ring went the pony; faster and faster it raced, but it could not dislodge the young rider. Then it reared and shied and kicked; still Ulysses sat as steady as if he had been glued to the pony's back. But the clown was determined he would not lose the wager. So he picked up a monkey and put it on the pony. Scampering up the boy's back, the monkey stood on Ulysses' shoulders, with its paws tugging at his hair. Around the ring dashed the pony with its two passengers, and the crowd burst into applause as the fearless lad again proved he could hold his mount. Even with the monkey clawing at him, Ulysses would not leave the pony's back until the clown handed him his five-dollar prize.

Shortly after Ulysses entered West Point, he was conceded to be the strongest rider at the Academy. "It was as good as any circus to see Grant ride," remarked a fellow cadet. "There was a dark bay horse that was so fractious that it was about to be condemned . . . Grant selected it for his horse. He bridled, mounted, and rode it every day at parade; and how he did ride! He handled the refractory creature as a giant would a child. The whole class would stand around admiring his wonderful command of the beast and his graceful evolutions."

Grant was also the Academy's top jumper, and he set a record that stood for a quarter of a century. General James B. Fry, then a candidate for admission to West

Point, told of watching Grant jump at the final mounted exercise of his graduating class. "The riding-master placed the leaping-bar higher than a man's head and called out 'Cadet Grant.' A clean-faced, slender, blue-eyed young fellow, weighing one hundred and twenty pounds, dashed from the ranks on a powerfully built chestnut-sorrel horse and galloped down the opposite side of the hall. As he turned at the farther end and came into the stretch across which the bar was placed, the horse increased his pace, and measuring his strides for the great leap before him, bounded into the air and cleared the bar, carrying his rider as if man and beast had been welded together. The spectators were speechless. 'Very well done, sir!' growled old Hershberger, the riding-master, and the class was dismissed and disappeared; but Cadet Grant remained a living image in my memory."

Other Presidents, although they did not set any records on horseback, thoroughly enjoyed riding. James Madison kept at least seven horses in the Washington stable and many more at his Montpelier plantation. James Monroe and John Quincy Adams were enthusiastic riders, and frail James K. Polk had practically no other diversion. Zachary Taylor was especially fond of riding his war horse, Old Whitey, and the White House stable attracted many visitors when Old Rough and Ready and Old Whitey moved to Washington. Even the more recent Presidents, who were less dependent on horses for transportation, frequently rode in their youth.

Franklin D. Roosevelt was particularly devoted to the sport. Beginning as a tot on a tiny Welsh pony, he continued to ride for enjoyment until he was stricken by polio.

At least one Chief Executive, William Howard Taft, turned to horseback as a means of losing weight. But usually the horse had much more exercise than he did. When Taft was governor of the Philippines, he became seriously ill. Concerned by the news, Secretary of War Elihu Root sent him a telegram inquiring about his condition. Taft received the telegram at a mountain resort to which he had traveled, partly on horseback. He replied that he felt much better and added: "Stood trip well, rode horseback twenty-five miles to five thousand feet elevation." When Root got his wire, he cabled back immediately: "Referring to your telegram — how is the horse?"

John Adams, who was still taking long rides at the age of seventy-eight, recognized the healthful effects of this type of exercise. "Rise and mount your horse by the morning's dawn, and shake away, amidst the great and beautiful scenes of nature that appear at that time of day, all the crudities that are left in your stomach, and all the obstructions that are left in your brains." Jefferson also praised horseback riding as an exercise, and he rode religiously every day until within a few weeks of his death. When he was seventy-six years old, he wrote a friend, "I am too feeble to walk much, but ride without fatigue six or eight miles a day and sometimes thirty or forty."

The present occupant of the White House, Lyndon Johnson, also is fond of riding. For vacations he returns to his LBJ ranch, where he can wear cowboy clothes, complete with a Texas-style hat, and climb back in the saddle. His ranch, which covers about 400 acres, is 65 miles west of Austin. Johnson frequently rides over his mesquite-covered land, partly for relaxation and partly to inspect his large herds of cattle.

Warren Harding, on the other hand, practically gave up riding after he reached the White House. He delighted in the sport but believed that it caused too much commotion for the man who was President. When one day his doctor urged him to ride for exercise, he replied, "If I could throw a blanket on the horse as I used to do on the farm, if I did not have to put on a special uniform and be followed by a staff of service men, I should like to ride."

Most of our recent Chief Executives also have felt that attending horse races was not a suitable Presidential pastime. But this was not true in earlier times. President Jefferson, who had closely followed the races at Williamsburg as a youth, was an avid track fan. It was said that he could never pass by a race course without stopping to enjoy the exhiliration of the event. A disgruntled Boston preacher noted that during Jefferson's administration between three and four thousand persons turned out for the Washington races, including "black and white and yellow, of all conditions, from the President of the United States to the beggar in his rags . . ." Jefferson liked to canter about at the track, paying his respects to the distinguished guests whose horses and carriages ringed the racing field. Often he would stop for a visit with James Madison, who shared his enthusiasm for the sport and owned part interest in a race horse.

John Quincy Adams never missed an opportunity to attend the races. He found that these outings offered a good excuse to escape from the throngs of visitors who wanted to see him. "This was the third day of the races, and Mrs. Adams was so far recovered as to go upon the grounds," he recorded in his diary on October 27, 1826. "It was a beautiful autumnal day. The races relieved me from many visitors."

Although Washington may not have attended races during his administration, in earlier years he frequently visited various tracks. On one occasion, he mentioned in his diary, his plantation work was rather disorganized, and he blamed this on a nearby race meeting. One track, Accotink, was only four miles from Mount Vernon, and Washington was one of its chief patrons. He also attended races at the Annapolis track, where for a while he was secretary of the Jockey Club. The Father of Our Country bet moderately on the races, and he carefully recorded in his diary the amounts he won and lost.

At least a few times Washington entered his own horses in races. His diary tells of him paying a man twelve shillings to ride one of his horses in a purse race at Accotink. But the most famous race occurred in 1788 when Washington pitted his prize Arabian stallion, Magnolia, against a roan colt owned by Jefferson. This was probably the only time in our history when the horses of two future Presidents competed in a match race. Washington's thoroughbred was the loser, which may have been the reason why soon afterward Magnolia was traded to Light-Horse Harry Lee, the father of the famous Civil War general.

Grant was another President who liked racing. When he was a young Army officer stationed in Detroit, he bought a small coal-black harness mare which he hitched to a buggy. Grant enjoyed racing other buggies down the crowded Detroit streets. Once he made a wager with a friend that his mare could carry him and another passenger a mile down busy Jefferson Avenue in less than three minutes. Grant won the bet, pocketed the fifty dollars, and then proceeded to "bestow affectionate caresses upon his horse, and after seeing her well cared for," invited his friends to a tavern to celebrate.

Of all our Chief Executives the one who was best known for horse racing was Andrew Jackson. At his Hermitage plantation he developed a string of swift steeds from the best Virginia and North Carolina stock. Whenever he had the time, Jackson personally trained his own thoroughbreds. "He worked a horse to the limit of endurance," wrote Marquis James, his biographer, "but somehow implanted in the animal a will to win, a

circumstance which epitomizes the character and eluci-
dates the singular attainment of Andrew Jackson."

Few turfmen were better judges of horses than Jackson, and this was proved when he purchased Truxton,
his most famous horse. Jackson decided to buy the large
bay stallion shortly after he watched it lose a race to a
fleet-footed gray gelding named Greyhound. Feeling
that Truxton had been defeated because of poor con-
ditioning, he began to retrain the horse carefully. Day
after day Truxton worked out on the track, with Jackson
driving the stallion harder and harder. Finally, when he
felt his horse was ready, Jackson challenged the owner
of Greyhound to a return match.

Greyhound was favored, not only because of his impressive record, but also because bettors thought Jackson
had worn Truxton out. But Jackson, his relatives, and
his racing cronies did not agree! Besides the original bet
of $5000, the master of the Hermitage put up land, store
supplies, horses, and slaves — and, in addition, made an
unusual side bet of $1500 worth of clothes. One of his
friends bet on Truxton all his money, his own horse, and,
recklessly, fifteen horses that did not belong to him!
Jackson's wife, Rachel, and his niece even bet their
gloves and sidesaddles.

Interest in the match was at the boiling point, and the
Tennessee farmers wagered money, crops, and land,
mostly on the popular Greyhound. "No contest on the
soil of Tennessee has ever been so exciting or caused so
much betting, considering the means of the people, as

this race," commented one turf historian. People came from neighboring Kentucky, Alabama, and Tennessee to see the great match.

The race was to be run in two out of three heats. Truxton set out like a streak of lightning, and, much to the amazement and chagrin of Greyhound's many backers, won two straight heats handily. Jackson and his friends collected their winnings and then held a joyous celebration.

Truxton later was matched against an unbeaten stallion named Ploughboy. Disaster struck the Jackson stable two days before the race when Truxton went lame. The thigh on one of its hind legs was badly swollen, and friends urged the general to postpone the race. When Jackson refused, even his most ardent followers doubted Truxton's ability to stand the strain of running two or three heats on a bad leg.

The two horses trotted to the starting line and were off at the tap of a drum. Ploughboy took an early lead, but Truxton caught up and won the first heat going away. Instead of celebrating, Jackson's friends grew gloomier, for Truxton had gone lame in a foreleg and had thrown a shoe on still a third leg. The pessimists predicted Truxton would be badly beaten in the last two heats. Jackson worked feverishly on Truxton's legs in the half hour between heats. The big champion returned to the starting line and ran well enough to beat Ploughboy by a convincing sixty yards.

In describing this race some years later, Jackson wrote

in *The American Farmer,* . . . "to crown the much doubted speed of Truxton with his opponents, he beat, on only two sound legs . . . the celebrated Ploughboy, who was never before beaten, and beating him without the assistance of whips or spurs. It is now no longer difficult for the numerous concourse of people who were present on that day to say 'whether or not Truxton be the true bred racer.' Truxton's winnings . . . amount to at least twenty thousand dollars, and his colts are not inferior to any on the continent."

After Jackson became President his racing affairs were managed by his nephew, Andrew Jackson Donelson. Old Hickory revamped the White House stable at considerable cost, kept up with promising Hermitage colts through letters, and raced three of his White House fillies under Donelson's name. None of them won any important races, but Jackson frequently went to the track.

In the spring of 1834 Jackson attended the races with his Vice President, Martin Van Buren. They stood and watched as two handlers held a large stallion named Busirus while the jockey mounted. When the men let go, the jockey could not control the horse, which bucked and charged against a fence. Jackson sprang in front of Van Buren and yelled, "Get behind me, Mr. Van Buren! They will run over you, sir." When Busirus finally was calmed down, Jackson scolded his trainer for not handling him correctly. Some of Van Buren's political rivals used the incident to illustrate their belief that Van Buren stood in the fatherly shadow of Old Hickory.

Except for the fillies that Donelson raced for him in Washington, Jackson's thoroughbreds seldom lost. There was one horse, however, he never could defeat, a mare named Maria. Truxton had been retired before Maria began to race, but Truxton's son, Decatur, tried to catch the mare and failed. Time and time again horses that were owned or backed by Jackson ran against Maria, but none of them was victorious. In 1837, when Jackson was an old man, a friend asked him if he had ever attempted anything that ended in failure. "Nothing that I can remember," said Old Hickory, "except Maria. I could not beat her."

While Jackson was in the White House, a friend gave him a wondrous sulky to use for traveling around Washington. A poet of that era, N. P. Willis, described it: "Some eccentric mechanic has presented President Jackson with a sulky made of rough cut hickory, with the bark on. It has very much of the everlasting look of 'Old Hickory' himself, and if he could be seen driving a high-stepping, bony old iron-gray stud in it, any passenger would see that there was as much fitness in the whole thing as in the chariot of Bacchus . . . Some curiously-twisted and gnarled branches have been ingeniously turned into handles and whip-box, and the vehicle is compact and strong."

Jackson's rough-hewn sulky was quite different from

the elegant carriages that most of our Presidents drove
in. Washington started the precedent of having an
elaborate equipage. The carriage he rode in for state
occasions was probably the most magnificent vehicle in
the country. It had a cream-colored body and was richly
decorated with gold medallions, painted panels depict-
ing the four seasons, green Venetian blinds, glossy black
leather upholstery, and the family coat of arms upon the
doors. His footmen and coachmen dressed in brilliant
white-and-scarlet liveries. Two outriders waited until
the President entered the coach, then leaped to their
saddles and rode on ahead, while the secretaries followed the Presidential carriage in a less elegant vehicle.

Washington considered that this splendid equipage
was in keeping with the dignity of his high office. But
it was criticized by some citizens as "too pompous for a
Republican president." Newspapers carried articles both
attacking and defending the President's luxurious carriage and the elaborate ceremony that accompanied his
travel. Even Mrs. John Adams felt called upon to say
that President Washington's equipage was "no more
state than is perfectly consistent with his station." But,
as for her own husband, she explained that "the Vice
President ten times to one goes to [the] Senate in a one-
horse chaise."

Martin Van Buren was also ridiculed for his lavish
equipage. A Washington paper tartly reported: "Mr.
Van Buren, although a Republican of the democratic
species, according to himself and friends, has no pre-

dominating taste for republican habits and fashions. His dinners have been the frequent as well as the most aristocratic of any which have been given during the session; and he drives no republican carriage but an aristocratic vehicle built either in Russia, or in the latest Russian model, drawn by a pair of superb trotters, which carry him to the Capitol, or any similar distance from his residence (about a mile and a half) in four minutes."

Of the later Presidents Chester Alan Arthur probably had the most splendid array of carriages and horses. He frequently rode in a favorite landau, which is a carriage with folding tops at front and rear. It was painted a dark green trimmed with red. The cushions and doors were faced with exquisite lace; the harness was heavily mounted with silver; the dark green dress blankets and coachman's lap robe were ornamented with the President's monogram. Inside the landau was a lap robe of Labrador otter, handsomely lined with green silk, and bearing the monogram "C.A.A." worked in silk. To draw the carriage Arthur obtained two perfectly matched horses of dark mahogany color.

Homespun Abraham Lincoln, on the the other hand, was not anxious to have an expensive equipage when he moved to 1600 Pennsylvania Avenue. Back in Illinois he had ridden in a ramshackle, one-horse buggy that had tires bound on with hickory bark. But after their arrival in Washington, Mrs. Lincoln insisted on owning a fine closed carriage. The President let his wife have her way, and he had to pay fourteen hundred dollars for the coach she ordered. When the rather ornate new carriage was delivered at the White House door, Lincoln described it as the slickest glass hack in town.

Grant, like Lincoln, was not interested in pompous carriages. He much preferred to ride in a small buggy behind a team of fast trotters. One day he was driving his horses along Washington's busy M Street at a speed faster than the law permitted when a policeman spotted him. The mounted officer galloped alongside the buggy and made its owner stop. When he recognized the man inside, the embarrassed policeman apologized profusely. "Officer, do your duty," replied Grant cheerfully. He was pleased instead of offended over the incident, and later he wrote a letter commending the policeman who had arrested the President.

8

In Swimming

A SMOOTH coconut shell sat on the late President John Kennedy's desk in the White House. Crudely carved into its side are the words, "Native knows posit he can pilot 11 alive need small boat Kennedy." The story behind this strange message on the coconut shell dates back to the Second World War when Kennedy, as a young naval officer, was stationed with a PT–boat squadron in the South Pacific.

On the night of August 2, 1943, his boat, PT–109, was patrolling Blackett Strait in the Solomon Islands, with a crew of thirteen aboard. A Japanese destroyer appeared suddenly out of the darkness and rammed PT–109, splitting it in half and causing it to burst into flames. Sailors on nearby PT–boats saw the crash and assumed everyone aboard had been killed.

Two enlisted men never were seen again, but Kennedy and ten others of his crew survived. The young skipper had wrenched his back when the impact knocked him to the deck, but he swam about one hundred yards to a badly burned sailor named McMahon and towed him back to the still-floating half of the wrecked boat. At daybreak the survivors decided they would have to

abandon the sinking hulk and swim to the nearest un-
occupied island. But McMahon's burns had made his
legs useless. So while the others made their own way,
Kennedy held McMahon's life preserver strap in his
teeth and pulled his companion three miles to the island.
The arduous swim took more than four hours.

Frantically the survivors tried in vain to flag down an
American vessel. On the third day Kennedy and his men
moved to an island nearer the frequently traveled Fergu-
son Passage. He again towed McMahon with the life-
belt strap between his teeth. This time the exhausting
swim lasted about three hours. Afterward Kennedy was
picked up by Solomon Island natives who paddled him
in their canoe to the island of Nauru. There he carved
the message on the coconut, which was carried to the
American sailors who finally rescued the stranded men.

Almost nineteen years later, on February 8, 1962, the
regular parade of visitors through the White House included Mr. and Mrs. Harry G. Fair and their four children. The Fairs had been designated as the nation's
"Scouting Family of the Year." President Kennedy was
presented a Boy Scout mile-swim card, and he read the
inscription aloud: "This is to certify that John Fitzgerald
Kennedy swam a full mile under safe conditions."
People in the room broke into laughter over the "safe
conditions," for the card was backdated to August 2,
1943.

Kennedy had been a superb swimmer since childhood,
mainly because of the relentless determination of his

father. "Even when we were six and seven years old," recalled the President's sister Eunice, "Daddy always entered us in public swimming races in the different age categories so we didn't have to swim against each other. And he did the same thing with us in sailing races. And if we won, he got terribly enthusiastic. Daddy was always very, very competitive. The thing he always kept telling us was that coming in second was just no good. The important thing was to win . . ."

The competitive drive instilled in him by his father carried over to Kennedy's swimming career at Harvard. His college roommate, Torbert Macdonald, told of the time Jack was to compete against Dick Tregaskis for the right to swim in the Yale meet. But Jack came down with influenza several days before the trial race and was confined to the campus infirmary.

"He was on a light diet at the infirmary because of his fever and this worried him," Macdonald said. "He was afraid he wouldn't be strong enough to win the swimming trials. So he made me smuggle malted milks and steaks into the infirmary. Then he'd get me to help him disappear from his room for an hour. He would rush to the Indoor Athletic Building, swim several laps in the pool, and rush back to the infirmary so that he would be back in bed before the nurse came around to take his temperature and give him his medicine."

When Kennedy was discharged from the hospital, he had not missed many days of practice. But he was weakened by his illness, and the coveted honor of swimming against Yale was won by Tregaskis. A few years later both Harvard swimmers gained fame in World War II — Tregaskis as author of the best-selling *Guadalcanal Diary* and Kennedy as the strong-swimming hero of PT–109.

Many Presidents were excellent swimmers, but none performed feats to match Kennedy's in the South Pacific. Zachary Taylor, however, was an aquatic hero on at least one occasion. In 1801, at the age of seventeen, he was amusing himself with some friends on the Kentucky side of the Ohio River. It was March and the big river was filled with large, dangerous ice chunks swirling in the strong current. One of the boys dared Taylor to try to swim across the treacherous river. Despite warnings from the others, Taylor plunged into the water and threaded his way between blocks of ice to the Indiana shore.

Unexpected dunkings were more the rule than heroic swims. As a boy, Ulysses S. Grant almost lost his life while he was fishing from floating logs with a playmate named Daniel Ammen. The log Grant was on suddenly rolled, throwing him into the water. His head struck another log, and the blow stunned him. Seeing the accident, young Ammen rushed over to rescue his friend. In the years that followed, these fishing companions both had distinguished military careers. Grant became the North's Civil War hero, and Ammen became an admiral.

John Quincy Adams, an exceptionally strong swimmer even when he reached old age, once nearly drowned in the Potomac River. While he lived in the White House, it was his habit to take a dip in the river almost every day. On June 13, 1825, Adams, his son John, and their servant, Antoine Giusta, decided to swim the Potomac where it was a mile wide. Adams and Antoine were to paddle to the far shore in an old canoe and then swim back. The son, who felt the canoe was unsafe, agreed to swim out halfway and meet them. This was in the days before bathing suits became popular, and men generally preferred to swim without any clothing. Antoine stripped completely, but the President set out on the excursion wearing pantaloons, a shirt, and a hat.

The combination of a leaky canoe and an unexpected squall caused a sudden change of plans midway across the river. The canoe began sinking, and the two men decided to abandon it. Just before Adams plunged into the water, he gave the servant his hat. Antoine, with no clothes to hinder him, made it easily to the Virginia shore, carrying the President's hat. Adams, who was weighted down by the pantaloons and loose sleeves of his shirt, found the going much more difficult. When he finally made it to safety, he was out of breath.

Antoine donned the President's soggy shirt and pantaloons and went to fetch a carriage. Meanwhile, the younger Adams grew impatient and swam across to the Virginia side. He found his father, and they basked naked in the sun until the carriage came. When they returned to the Executive Mansion hours later, Adams listed his losses as one shoe, one coat, one waistcoat, two napkins, and two handkerchiefs. After this hazardous swimming experience, the President admitted that while he had been "struggling for life and gasping for breath," he had "ample leisure to reflect upon my own indiscretion."

William McKinley also had a close call in the water. As a boy he could not swim and once got beyond his depth in Ohio's Mosquito Creek. An older boy tried to save him and almost drowned himself. Finally a third youth came to the rescue and pulled them both out.

James A. Garfield's dreams of a career as a sailor were almost translated into a watery death when he fell off a canal boat. Shortly after the youthful Garfield took a job on the vessel, he became sick with fever. But he continued working despite his illness. While fastening a rope at the rear of the boat, he became dizzy and fell into the water. Luckily, he clutched the rope that was trailing in the water, and fellow deck hands hauled him back aboard. Garfield could not swim at the time, and he might never have been rescued if he had not been able to grab the rope.

"That first trip," wrote Garfield years later, "was one of many adventures. I could not swim a particle and I knew almost nothing about the water except what I had read. The consequence was I fell into the canal just fourteen times and had fourteen almost miraculous escapes from drowning . . ."

The specter of drowning never bothered Theodore Roosevelt. One wintry day at Oyster Bay, New York, a woman saw a swimmer far from shore bobbing in the waves. She ran up to a clam digger, begging him to get his boat and save the poor drowning man. The clam digger slowly looked up from his shovel, glanced out to sea, and said, "Hell, lady, he's in no danger, it's only Roosevelt."

A walk with Teddy Roosevelt often turned into a mountain-climbing, channel-swimming ordeal. On one such jaunt the walking party came to a large pond. Roosevelt placed his watch and money in his hat and plunged in, clothes and all. His companions, some wearing expensive suits, had to follow. "What difference does it make?" asked Teddy. "It was the shortest, quickest way, and a wetting does no harm."

When Roosevelt and his friends hiked around Washington, their path often led them to Rock Creek or the Potomac River. The President described one Rock Creek dip: "The ice had just broken and the creek was a swollen flood, running like a millrace. We did the usual climbing stunts at the various rocks, and then swam the creek and it was a good swim, in our winter clothes and hobnail boots and the icy current running really fast."

"If we swam the Potomac," Roosevelt said, "we usually took off our clothes. I remember one such occasion when the French ambassador, Jusserand, who was a member of the Tennis Cabinet, was along, and, just as we were about to get in to swim, somebody said, 'Mr. Ambassador, Mr. Ambassador, you haven't taken off your gloves,' to which he promptly responded, 'I think I will leave them on; we might meet ladies!"

Roosevelt's nude swimming caused him embarrassment in 1876, shortly before he began his studies at Harvard. He started at five one morning to row across Oyster Bay to see a girl friend. He arrived at eight, decided it was too early to call, and stretched out on a rock to sleep. When he awoke he discovered that his rowboat had drifted into the bay. So he doffed his clothes and swam out to retrieve it. Then he left his clothes in the boat and fell asleep again, this time under the dock.

Teddy snoozed peacefully until he was awakened by voices and footsteps on the wooden planks above. Sitting up with a start, the young man was horrified to find that the rowboat, with his clothes, had drifted away again. To make the matter worse, his girl friend and a companion were waiting on the dock. They stood there for what seemed to Roosevelt an eternity before finally walking off into the woods. Teddy found his boat up a creek and rowed home without stopping to see the girl friend who unwittingly had made him feel foolish.

Old Virginia records tell that two women stole George Washington's clothes while he was swimming in the Rappahannock in the summer of 1751. The women were arrested and convicted. One turned state's evidence, and the other received fifteen lashes on her bare back. Washington, however, had sailed to Barbados before the trial began.

There is a legend about John Quincy Adams also being stranded without his clothes. According to the story, an enterprising female journalist, Anne Royall, was having difficulty getting Adams to submit to an interview. So she carefully studied the President's daily habits to figure out some scheme for finding him alone. Her research provided this one promising bit of information — Adams was accustomed to go, unaccompanied, to the Potomac every morning, strip off his clothes, and take a swim in the river.

Before dawn one day Adams walked to the river, shed his coat and pantaloons as usual, and leaped in. Miss Royall came along minutes later. She sat down on the President's clothes and called for him to come in closer. Realizing his predicament, Adams swam in far enough so that just his head was above water. Miss Royall had the President at her mercy, and he was forced to answer her questions before she would leave.

Fortunately, our recent Chief Executives have been spared the embarrassment that could result from swimming nude in rivers and streams. The White House now is equipped with a long, narrow swimming pool, heated to allow year-around use. Shortly after Franklin D. Roosevelt came into office, the New York *Daily News* asked permission of the President and Congress to launch a money-raising campaign for a White House swimming pool. Permission was granted, and the *Daily News,* together with more than a dozen other papers around the nation, solicited the public for contributions. Within a short time, forty thousand dollars was collected to build an excellent pool and dressing rooms.

"It is the only health builder that any President of the U.S. will find in the White House," said one of Roosevelt's friends. "All else that I know anything else about is decidedly destructive."

F.D.R. used the pool almost every evening. Following his physician's orders, he quit work at five-thirty to take an hour-long swim before dinner. He could not use his paralyzed legs, but his shoulder, back, and arm muscles were so well developed that he could outswim most members of his staff. "When skylarking in the pool the most powerful swimmers had to be cautious of grappling with him," said a White House aide, "for he could duck any of them with a half-nelson few men could throw off."

Neither Harry Truman nor Dwight Eisenhower shared Roosevelt's enthusiasm for swimming. The unathletic Harry Truman, who had learned to swim in his forties, referred to the White House pool, in homespun fashion, as his "swimming hole." He used a side stroke and always kept his head above water to avoid losing his glasses. Preferring to exercise outdoors, Dwight Eisenhower seldom used the White House pool until the latter part of his first term in office. But after he suffered his heart attack, his doctors persuaded him to swim for thirty minutes at noon each day, with the water temperature put up to 86–90 degrees.

When Kennedy replaced Eisenhower in the mansion on Pennsylvania Avenue, he was given a personal tour of his new home by the outgoing President. Showing

Kennedy the swimming pool, Ike said, "I just thought you would like to see what is available around here for exercise." Kennedy found the pool to his liking, and he began the practice of taking a daily dip with David Powers, a White House aide. Powers informed newsmen that there was only one important rule for swimming with the President: "All you've got to do is keep your head above water so you can talk."

Lyndon Johnson also enjoys this type of exercise, and he frequently uses the White House pool. When vacationing in Texas he swims in a large outdoor pool on his LBJ ranch. It is permanently heated, so that President Johnson and his guests can take a refreshing dip even in the cold winter weather. Music is piped into the area for the swimmers' pleasure, and near the pool are several telephones that keep the President in close touch with news from all over the world.

Another famous Presidential bathing place was the mineral springs pool at Warm Springs, Georgia. There Franklin D. Roosevelt made a courageous effort to conquer the effects of polio that had crippled him in August, 1921. F.D.R. paid his first visit to Warm Springs in 1924, on the advice of George Foster Peabody, half-owner of the health resort. The dilapidated main building and surrounding cottages were unappealing, but the warm water, rich in magnesium and calcium, greatly impressed Roosevelt. He wrote to Peabody, "Every morning I spend two hours in the most wonderful pool in the world, and it is no exaggeration to say that the muscles in my legs have improved to an extent noticeable in every way."

He returned to Warm Springs in 1925 and again the following year. Newspaper and magazine articles began telling about the remote place in the Georgia pinewoods where the prominent New Yorker was struggling to overcome his physical handicap. Roosevelt's enthusiasm for Warm Springs was contagious, and soon crippled persons in every part of the country were eager to visit the health resort. In 1926 F.D.R. decided to purchase the Warm Springs spa. Incorporating it as a non-profit organization, he invested much of his own money in improving and expanding the facilities. But as the spa grew in popularity, its operating expenses also increased sharply. It was not until the President's Birthday Ball in 1934 netted more than one million dollars for the foundation that Warm Springs was placed on sound financial footing.

Roosevelt was a happy man when he could play like a walrus in the Warm Springs water. He also had fun teaching other cripples to swim and exercise. For those who could not use conventional swimming strokes, he invented new ones and gave them titles such as the "floating mare," "swooning swan," and "popping porpoise." The "happy irregulars," as F.D.R. called the Warm Springs patients, even formed a water polo team that played against the medical staff. In these rousing games the future President of the United States turned in some sterling performances at left halfback.

Swimming helped Roosevelt to be optimistic about his chances for recovery, despite the fact that he never regained any significant use of his legs. Vice Admiral Ross T. McIntire, his White House physician, recalled, "As the years went by I knew that his bright expectations of recovery would never be fulfilled. Was it a kindness not to tell him the truth?

"I discovered the answer at one of his last swims in the White House pool. As he churned up and down the length of the pool, his powerful arms and shoulders pulled him swiftly through the water with strong, steady strokes. His limp lower limbs, as always, trailed uselessly behind. Afterward he heaved himself up to a sitting position on the side. 'That was wonderful!' he said exultantly. 'These days I can feel distinct new tremors in three of my left toes! See!'

"All I could see was that his feet were shifting gently in the buoyant water. Yet, I nodded. Only a fool, which F.D.R. was not, deceives himself. If he felt tremors, they were surely there.

"They were tremors of hope. It was the same courage to fight on that he had given so many others."

9

At the Helm

THE romance of the sea, with exotic ports of call, legends of buried pirate booty and fiery naval battles, had long excited boyhood spirits. Even a boy who might fulfill his parents' dreams and grow up to be President of the United States could be tempted by the ocean's lure.

George Washington's older brother, Laurence, was a midshipman in the British Navy. He encouraged George to follow a similar career and got him a sea chest and a midshipman's warrant. The youth, however, needed no prodding; the daring adventures of a sailor's life greatly appealed to him. Often he would stand on the banks of the Potomac River, staring fondly at passing ships and yearning for the time when he could go to sea. But his uncle in England wrote to his mother and convinced her that George should not join the British Navy. She pleaded with her son to give up the notion of becoming a sailor, and young Washington reluctantly agreed to follow her advice.

When Laurence became ill in the fall of 1751, his doctor suggested that a trip to the island of Barbados might help him regain his health. George, not yet twenty, accompanied his brother on the ocean voyage.

Their ship left the mouth of the Potomac on September 28, 1751. By the time they reached Barbados, George had nearly mastered the art of sailing and could identify almost every type of ship they passed. His log revealed the voyage was anything but smooth. "This morning arose with agreeably assurances of a certain and steady trade Wind," he wrote, "which after nearly five Weeks buffiting and being toss'd by a fickle and Merciless ocean was glad'ening knews."

James Garfield made his boyhood ambition of being a sailor come true, at least for a short time. In 1877, three years before his election to the Presidency, he recalled his youthful ambition. "I formed the determination to become a sailor," he explained. "Nautical novels did it. I had read a large number of them, all I could get in the neighborhood. My mother tried to turn my attention in other directions, but the books were considered bad and from that very fact were fascinating. I remember especially the 'Pirates Own Book' which became a sort of Bible or general authority with me at that period."

When young Garfield was hired as a hand on a canal boat, he discovered that all sailors did not have the enjoyable experiences he had read about. You recall that on his first trip he got into a savage fight with a bully and also fell into the canal fourteen times, almost drowning each time. Moreover, the work was hard and tedious, and the canal boat stopped at such ports as Akron and Cuyahoga Falls, which were hardly exotic, exciting places. Although he was promoted to the job of bowsman after his first round trip, he soon decided that some other career would be more to his liking.

A swollen creek near Abilene, Kansas, provided Dwight Eisenhower and his brother Edgar a whirling boat ride that also could have ended in a drowning. Exploring the flooded waters when their mother thought they were doing their chores, the young brothers happened upon a flat-bottomed boat and could not resist the temptation to take a ride.

Whooping with delight but unable to steer the frail little craft, Ike and Edgar sped down the creek toward the turbulent Smoky Hill River. Their mother meanwhile missed them and sent the other Eisenhower brothers to hunt for the lost boys. No trace of the missing pair was uncovered, so Ike's father was called home from work, and he organized a full-scale search. The hunt ended when a cowboy spotted the boat just as it was about to be carried into the raging river. Fearing that the craft would soon be overturned in the swirling waters, he hurriedly tossed the boys his lasso and called to them, "Catch!" Ike grabbed the end of the rope, and the cowboy hauled the frightened boys to shore.

John Kennedy and his older brother Joe were much more experienced sailors than the Eisenhowers, but they were just as daring. They started sailing alone when they were so small that their boat looked empty from the shore. As schoolboys the Kennedy brothers entered many boat races during their summer vacations at Hyannis Port, Massachusetts. Before the start of one regatta the officials and most participants agreed that the strong wind and rough water would make sailing that day too dangerous. But Joe and Jack were determined that the race should be held, and they pushed off in their little boat. The churning sea whipped their tiny craft mercilessly, and within a few hundred yards from the dock both boys fell into the water. Before any of the startled onlookers could reach them, the brothers swam back to their drifting craft and pulled it in to shore. They still pleaded for the chance to race, but the cautious officials canceled the regatta.

The boys' father, Joseph Kennedy, Senior, was determined that his children should be outstanding in water sports. He taught them all, including his daughters, to swim and sail. The family boat was appropriately called *The Ten of Us*, and a later boat was named *One More*. In boat races, as in other sports, the Kennedy children learned from their father never to be satisfied with anything short of victory. The will to win was such an important family creed that Joe and Jack were sent away from the dinner table one night because their father felt they had not tried hard enough in a sailboat race.

The Kennedy boys continued sailing when they entered college. To unfurl the sails and guide a skiff over the choppy blue waters was their favorite form of recreation. Moreover, Joe and Jack practiced the art of seamanship until they became expert. Together with a friend they piloted the boat that won the coveted Mc-Millan Cup for Harvard in 1938. The two eldest Kennedy brothers were close companions, and after Joe was killed in the Second World War, Jack edited a privately printed book about him entitled *As We Remember Joe.* In it he said, "I think if the Kennedy children amount to anything, now or ever amount to anything, it will be due more to Joe's behavior and his constant example than to any other factor."

Franklin D. Roosevelt was in love with boats, sailing, and the ocean all his life. His grandfather owned a fleet of sailing ships and was a distinguished sea captain. As a boy Franklin lived on a large estate at Hyde Park, New York, where he and playmate Edmund Rogers tried all sorts of ambitious projects. Once the boys chopped down a few trees and built a little fishing boat by a Hyde Park cove. On launching day they loaded it with all their fishing gear and happily set out for a day of adventure. But no sooner had they pushed away from the dock than the boat began to sink, soaking the boys and all their equipment. More successful was their imaginary sailing ship, which was a crudely built tree-house high in a hemlock. The pair took many exciting treetop voyages and never let a storm force them to drop anchor.

Roosevelt acquired his exceptional skill as a sailor in the waters around Campobello Island, two miles off the coast of Maine. His father built a cottage at Campobello in 1886, and Franklin thoroughly enjoyed his visits to the family summer home. He went there many times, as a child and later as an adult. It was during one of his vacations at Campobello, in 1921, that Roosevelt was struck by polio.

When he was young he would sail for hours, and his mother often would go along and read to him. Old photographs show Franklin steering his father's sloop, the *Half Moon*. The family later acquired another *Half Moon*, this one a sixty-foot, two-masted schooner. When he was sixteen Franklin received a gift that he put above all others — his own 21-foot sailboat, called the *New Moon*.

Roosevelt's keen interest in seamanship almost led him into a naval career. "I've always liked the Navy," he once admitted. "In fact, I only missed by a week going to Annapolis. I would have done so, only my parents objected." During the First World War, however, he did have the opportunity to work directly with sailors. He served under Woodrow Wilson as Assistant Secretary of the Navy, which was the same position that his cousin Theodore had held at the start of the Spanish-American War.

F. D. R. enjoyed his association with the Navy, but he craved more action than his desk job provided. His boss, Josephus Daniels, said, "I think he would have been happy if the offices of the Navy Department had been located on a battleship. Every time he had the opportunity, even for a week-end, he would make for a ship and he loved to have part in its navigation."

Roosevelt's son James remembered that his father

went to Campobello several times on Navy destroyers, once with the sailboat *Vireo* resting on the deck. He often persuaded the ship captains to let him take over at the helm. James said his father frightened the officers with his daring tactics, such as going through narrow fog-bound channels at full speed ahead. "The hapless skippers," explained the younger Roosevelt, "didn't know whether to defy the assistant secretary of the Navy then and there, or to risk court-martial later by allowing this wild man with the pince-nez and Harvard accent to pile up their ships. Even today, I occasionally meet a retired admiral who will regale me with a horrible account of one of those mad sails into Campobello with father giving the orders."

F.D.R.'s intimate knowledge of Campobello waters didn't help one night when he had to guide the *Half Moon* back to the island after picking up relatives at Eastport, Maine. The fog was so thick he had to hang a lantern on the main boom and use bell signals to tell his crew what speed he wanted. He was confident he could find his way back easily, but the boat barely missed some docks, came close to hitting a small island, and went completely off course. Roosevelt finally realized the iron lantern swinging from the boom had been attracting the ship's compass!

In September 1923, F.D.R. and an old school friend purchased a run-down houseboat for $3750 and renamed it the *Larooco*. After the craft was repaired, Roosevelt used it for Florida cruises. He liked to fish from its sides and take the boat into deserted beaches where he could exercise in the shallow water. In 1927 a hurricane battered the Florida coast, and the *Larooco* was swept into a grove of pine trees four miles inland. The houseboat was so badly damaged that it had to be sold for scrap. "So ended a good old craft with a personality," said F.D.R. "On the whole it was an end to be preferred to that of a gasoline barge . . ."

The most luxurious ship ever used by Roosevelt was the *Nourmahal*, a sleek white yacht built in Germany for Vincent Astor, his wealthy New York neighbor. The *New York Times* called it an "ocean liner in miniature . . . the biggest and fastest ocean-going motor yacht ever built . . ." F.D.R. went on an eleven-day trip to Miami and the Bahamas aboard the *Nourmahal* shortly after he was elected to his first term in the White House. Several other times the President took deep-sea fishing expeditions on this elegant yacht.

One of Roosevelt's most exciting voyages occurred in June 1933 when he set sail in a friend's schooner, *Amberjack II.* The plan was to cruise leisurely up the New England coast from Buzzards Bay to Campobello, giving the President the chance to relax en route. All went well until a savage "nor'-easter" struck Cape Cod just as F.D.R. was taking the ship into Nantucket Harbor. Soon the President was wet and shivering from the rain and sea spray, but he refused to turn the wheel over to anyone else. The twisting entrance to the harbor and the dangerous shoals rising near the surface of the water were the kinds of challenges that he relished.

Carefully executing a series of tricky sailing maneuvers, Roosevelt brought his ship through the narrow channel with no mishaps. His expert handling of the *Amberjack* amazed veteran seamen. "An ordinary yachtsman wouldn't have done it," said one observer. When invited ashore to rest after his exhausting performance, Roosevelt replied that he had no intention of setting foot on dry land for two weeks.

Roosevelt's love of the sea was reflected in the White House while he lived there. He had naval prints and paintings hung on the walls of his bedroom, in his executive wing office, and in the Oval Room. On his desk sat a ship's clock, a barometer, and a paperweight shaped like a ship's wheel. He also had an extensive collection of ship models on display. However, Secretary of the Interior Harold Ickes thought Roosevelt carried his devotion to the sea a bit too far when he called a Cabinet meeting aboard the *Indianapolis*. "I'm willing to die for the President," Ickes growled, "but I won't get seasick for him."

F.D.R.'s official Presidential yacht was the U.S.S. *Potomac,* a converted Coast Guard patrol boat. To make it over into a yacht, cabins and an elevator with a combined weight of thirty-nine tons were added topside. This made the boat roll badly when fully loaded and made it unsuitable for anything but sailing in protected waters. The gangplank had handrails so Roosevelt could haul himself aboard with little aid. Before the

Second World War, the President enjoyed cruises on the Potomac about two weekends a month. Aboard ship he whiled away the hours fishing, exploring the coves of Chesapeake Bay, and catching up on his mail.

Many Presidents used boats for travel, and, while not as enthusiastic as Roosevelt, they usually enjoyed their voyages. Andrew Jackson used to sail on the Potomac River to the Rip Raps, a sea-island summer resort off Norfolk, Virginia. In 1853 Millard Fillmore took his White House successor, Franklin Pierce, and famous author Washington Irving on a trip down the Potomac aboard the *Vixen* to inspect a new steamship.

During the Civil War Abraham Lincoln sailed on the *River Queen* to City Point, Virginia, at the request of General Ulysses S. Grant. The President later traveled on the *Malvern* to Richmond, shortly after that city had been taken by the Yankees. Guarded carefully by soldiers, he and an admiral then walked about a mile and a half to the mansion that had been occupied by Jefferson Davis, the head of the Confederacy.

When Grant became President, he sometimes took a boat to his vacation resort at Long Branch, New Jersey. His friends were miffed when critics objected to these short sea trips. "The Democratic papers," said one supporter, "forgetting Buchanan's trips on the *Harriet Lane,* and Andrew Johnson's excursions on the *Waywanda,* are abusing President Grant for going on the *Talapoosa* to Long Branch . . ."

More famous than any earlier ship was the U.S.S.

Mayflower, the official yacht of five Chief Executives —
Theodore Roosevelt, William Howard Taft, Calvin Coolidge, Warren Harding, and Herbert Hoover. The
Mayflower, originally built as a private vessel in the
1890's, became the floating White House in 1902. It was
outfitted with executive offices and handsomely decorated rooms for entertaining. When Taft became President, a marble oversized bathtub was installed in the
main bathroom.

Theodore Roosevelt, who did not hesitate to send the
fleet around the world, was not much of a sailing enthusiast and made infrequent use of the *Mayflower.* In
1904, however, he used it for a buffet luncheon for the
delegation to the Russo-Japanese treaty conference.
Since the President was trying to serve as the neutral
peacemaker between the warring Russians and Japanese,
he took every precaution to assure that the luncheon
went smoothly. He even gave the ship steward careful
instructions for seating his guests, making certain each
diplomat was assigned a place at the table in keeping
with his rank.

To Coolidge the luxurious *Mayflower* was almost a
second home. On weekends he liked to cruise down the
Potomac with a boatload of guests. As commander in
chief of the Navy, Coolidge received special honors
whenever he came aboard the yacht. The sailors would
all stand at attention, and the band would play the National Anthem. Then the steward would ceremoniously
hand the President his yachting cap. "Personally, I do

not like all this attention," Coolidge whispered one time
to an aunt, "but it is for the President of the United
States, and I have a great respect for the office."

In June 1927, Coolidge combined business and pleasure when he agreed to review part of the fleet while
cruising along the Virginia shore. The night before the
scheduled review the sea suddenly became very rough,
causing the *Mayflower* to swerve from side to side. Most
of the passengers, including Coolidge, were soon very
seasick. Throughout the night the rolling motion continued, and the next morning the President stayed in his
quarters until time for the review to begin. Then he
bravely gritted his teeth, donned his yachting cap,
grabbed his binoculars, and proceeded to take his place
for the ceremony. He stood dutifully at the bridge for
about thirty minutes, frequently saluting and posing for
photographs. But when the last battleship passed, Coolidge quickly retreated to his quarters and sank into a
sofa, feeling miserable. The seasick President, however,
could not even suffer in privacy, for a pesky photog-
rapher managed to snap a picture of him at the height
of his distress.

Harry Truman had at his disposal another Presidential
yacht, called the U.S.S. *Williamsburg*. This speedy,
oceangoing craft was launched in 1931 and used in the
Second World War as a command ship in the Atlantic.
It had quarters for twenty-four guests plus its own
barber and tailor shops. Several times Truman took the
yacht on vacation trips to Key West, Florida, and often

he used it for shorter voyages on the Potomac. Dwight Eisenhower, Truman's successor in the White House, took a few cruises on the *Williamsburg*, but during his administration he had the yacht decommissioned.

Eisenhower occasionally used a smaller yacht which he named the *Barbara Anne*, after his granddaughter. When Democrat John Kennedy took over the ninety-two-foot vessel in 1960, he quickly changed the name that his Republican predecessor had given it. He called the yacht the *Honey Fitz*, in honor of his maternal grandfather, John Fitzgerald, a famous Boston politician and also a Democrat. President Kennedy took advantage of every opportunity to slip away from his hectic job and sail serenely on the *Honey Fitz*. His interest in sailing had not waned since his college racing days. In 1962 he watched part of the famous America's Cup sailboat races near Newport, Rhode Island. His vantage point was the bow of the U.S.S. *Joseph P. Kennedy, Jr.,* named after his older brother.

President Lyndon Johnson in recent years has taken up boating as a hobby. He likes to pilot his motorboat up and down the Pedernales River that runs in front of his Texas ranch home. At times he takes longer excursions on the series of artificial lakes around the city of Austin.

In the days before motorboats and yachts were built, many Presidents used their own muscles to propel boats. When George Washington was twenty-two, he and several companions paddled down the Monongahela River to investigate French activities in the Ohio Valley. Thomas Jefferson as a boy liked to paddle across the Rivianna River to a quiet place where he could hunt or read the classics. William Henry Harrison did his boyhood canoeing on the historic James River.

Franklin Pierce, when he was the Democratic candidate for the Presidency in the summer of 1852, watched the first Yale-Harvard crew race. Many years later Franklin D. Roosevelt tried out for crew at Harvard, but the best he could do was earn the position of stroke on an intramural team. William Howard Taft was an oarsman on Yale's freshman crew, but his father discouraged him from going out for the varsity. No one, however, could discourage Theodore Roosevelt from rowing. Teddy relished the strenuous exercise of pulling the oars, and often he rowed for hours on end, stopping only long enough to enjoy a picnic luncheon at some secluded spot.

Sailing was much less appealing to Roosevelt because he regarded it as a "lazy man's sport," and motorboating held no fascination for him. "I suppose it sounds archaic," he declared, "but I cannot help thinking that the people with motor boats miss a great deal. If they would only keep to rowboats or canoes, and use oars or paddles themselves, they would get infinitely more benefit than by having their work done for them by gasoline."

Roosevelt practiced what he preached. He once rowed his wife sixteen miles and still felt fit as a fiddle when he finally pulled in his oars.

10

Keeping Fit

An early-morning visitor to the White House during the Coolidge administration could have beheld a strange sight. If he had been able to slip past the guards and into the private family quarters, he might have seen the President of the United States jiggling up and down on an electric horse. Coolidge, who shied away from most forms of physical exertion, enjoyed his daily rides on the mechanical steed. And he claimed that this form of exercise helped him keep hale and hearty.

But the electric horse caused its share of problems, too. A story was told about the first time that Coolidge, wearing a business suit and hat, cautiously mounted the contraption. He pressed the button and the horse suddenly reared. The President, not knowing how to handle the bucking bronco, lost his hat and almost fell off. Coolidge eventually mastered the art of staying in the saddle, but the mechanism now and then blew a fuse. An electrician's mate from the Navy yard told a reporter, "They're always sending someone up from the yard to fix it. He don't know how to change the gaits."

Several other Presidents tried various forms of exercise as a means of keeping fit. About ten years before he moved to the White House, Benjamin Harrison purchased a rowing machine that was guaranteed to provide a safe and pleasant workout. The advertiser's brochure for this machine is still preserved among President Harrison's papers. But there is no evidence regarding how often he used it, or whether he found it effective. Rutherford B. Hayes, on the other hand, was known to be consistent in his exercising. As a youth he began taking daily gymnastic workouts, and he continued this practice every morning during his term in the White House.

Dwight Eisenhower also became an expert gymnast after his knee injury took him out of football. He developed such strength in his arms that he could chin himself three times with one hand. And he learned how to do the giant swing, which is a difficult feat on the horizontal bar.

Franklin D. Roosevelt was another President who used gymnastic apparatus to help strengthen his arm muscles. After polio had left his legs nearly useless, Roosevelt worked out on parallel bars. Swinging his arms slowly forward, he was able to pull his paralyzed legs the full length of the bars.

Tall, lanky Abraham Lincoln was one of the most agile Chief Executives. As a youth it was said he could lean back from a standing position until his head would touch the floor. James Garfield must have been supple, too, if we can believe the statement of a doorkeeper at the White House. He told reporters he once saw the

President spring into the air, land on his hands, and without apparent effort turn a perfect handspring.

Some of our Presidents might have won blue ribbons if they had competed in a modern track meet. Hayes definitely would have earned a place on any Presidential track team, for he distinguished himself at Kenyon College as one of the school's champion runners. Washington, Jefferson, Jackson, and Lincoln were all reputed to have been fast of foot. John Quincy Adams may not have been as swift a runner, but while he was President he kept a mental record of how long it took him to jog around Capital Square each morning, and he competed with himself to better his own record.

A humorous story is told of a quarter-mile race that was held in Salisbury, North Carolina, between Andrew Jackson and a giant of a man named Hugh Montgomery. Jackson was considered the swiftest man in town and Montgomery the strongest. So Jackson gave Montgomery a head start of half the distance, while Montgomery had the handicap of having to carry a man on his back. Jackson took off like a flying comet, caught his opponent near the finish, and won the weird race by two or three yards. The only person in town who did not think the contest had been great fun was the man who had ridden on Montgomery's back. He had been squeezed so tightly and jolted so severely that he was out of breath and badly shaken when he finally crossed the finish line.

As a broadjumper, probably no other President could

have matched the ability of Washington. His legs and thighs were exceptionally powerful, and he could easily leap a brook that most other strong men could not span. When Washington was a boy and young adult, it was frequently said that he could outjump anyone who would challenge him. Much more modest claims as a jumper were made by Franklin D. Roosevelt. While a student at Groton, he wrote his mother, "I am going to try for the standing high, running high and standing broad jump, as well as the ten-yard dash and the potato race." Then he added realistically, "I do not expect to get a single thing." Roosevelt did, however, have something to boast about at Groton when he won the Class Three High Kick. Overjoyed by his accomplishment, he wrote home: "My kick was 7 feet 3½ inches from the floor . . . I kicked just 2 feet over my head."

While historians generally discredit the tale that Washington threw a dollar across the Rappahannock River, they do believe he may have accomplished this feat with a stone. The Father of our Country definitely could hold his own when it came to hurling stones or tossing iron bars. Charles Willson Peale, the noted artist who painted Washington's portrait, told of an afternoon when he and several young visitors at Mount Vernon were engaged in the sport of pitching the bar. Suddenly, Peale reported, Washington appeared among the group and asked to have the missile. "No sooner did the heavy iron bar feel the grasp of his mighty hand," said Peale, "than it lost the power of gravitation, and whizzed through the air, striking the ground far, very far, beyond our utmost limits. We were indeed amazed, as we stood around all stripped to the buff, with shirt sleeves rolled up, and having thought ourselves very clever fellows, while the Colonel, on retiring, pleasantly observed, 'When you beat my pitch, young gentlemen, I'll try again.'"

Washington also excelled at pitching quoits, which was a popular sport in Colonial times and continued to be played, particularly along the Atlantic seaboard, in the nineteenth century. In quoits a two-pound ring or flat stone was hurled a distance of about sixty feet at a pin called a "meg." To "ring the meg" repeatedly required both strength and skill. Besides Washington, a number of other Presidents, including Lincoln, whiled away spare hours by playing variations of this game. Jackson also enjoyed hurling objects at a target, and he was said to be a champion at throwing the "long bullet." This unusual sport involved hurling a heavy iron ball from a leather strap in such a way as to make it roll through a marked goal.

The popular game of horseshoes is closely related to quoits. Vice President John Tyler was playing horseshoes at his home in Virginia when a messenger rode up to him with the news that President Harrison had died. Herbert Hoover was another horseshoe fan. But it was Harry Truman who delighted the nation's millions of horseshoe enthusiasts when he ordered the construction of the first horseshoe court on the White House grounds.

President Truman was presented with some horseshoes plated with bronze and chromium, and he frequently invited intimate friends to join him in a game of trying to pitch ringers.

Other Presidents invited cronies to join them in their exercise, and sometimes the experience was much more rigorous than tossing horseshoes with Truman. Hoover played a strenuous game of medicine ball with Cabinet officers and other government officials every morning except Sunday. Summer or winter, rain or shine, for half an hour each day the aging, paunchy players would pass an eight-pound ball back and forth over a high net on the White House lawn. Reporters heard about these games, and soon the select group of Presidential companions came to be known as the Medicine-Ball Cabinet.

At first some of the Cabinet members, unaccustomed to so much exertion, were exhausted by the fast-paced workouts. But with daily practice they learned to take their extracurricular duty in stride. Following every game, unless it was raining or a heavy snow had recently fallen, a light breakfast was served under a magnolia tree. There the President and his ballplayers, all wrapped in heavy blankets, would chat amiably over grapefruit, toast, and coffee.

In addition to his opponents for boxing, wrestling, and jujitsu matches, Theodore Roosevelt engaged friendly rivals in bouts with the single-sticks. This was a type of fencing, in which tough heavy sticks were used instead of swords. The President's sparring partners were always men who were not afraid of absorbing some physical punishment. For even when a combatant warded off his opponent's strike, the blow from the collision of the sticks stung with its vibration. "Sometimes we hit hard," Roosevelt wrote a friend, "and today I have a bump over one eye and a swollen wrist."

Much better known were Teddy's tennis matches. Four other Presidents — William Howard Taft, Franklin D. Roosevelt, Dwight Eisenhower, and John Kennedy — all played tennis quite regularly at one time or another, but none of them achieved the fame on the court that came to Teddy. Although Roosevelt imposed a strict regulation that he never be photographed while playing tennis, there was no secret about the hectic games that took place behind the White House gates. Diplomats and politicians who had appointments with the President were made to wait until he had finished a rousing match on the court outside his office. Roosevelt played as often as possible, even on scorching hot days or when it rained so hard that the ball had practically lost its bounce. He loved the game because it offered the kind of ceaseless action and intense excitement he constantly craved.

The selection of Roosevelt's tennis companions was viewed by some as having political implications. While he played occasionally with other friends, the President generally drew his partners from a certain group of devoted young government officials. Some of these players, like Gifford Pinchot and James R. Garfield, became Teddy's close personal friends and trusted advisors. The newspapers began referring to the group as the Tennis Cabinet, and rumors circulated around Washington that any man with whom the President played tennis had a bright political future ahead.

Roosevelt's brand of tennis was completely unorthodox but surprisingly effective. He gripped the racket halfway up the handle with his index finger pushing along the back. Instead of throwing the ball into the air when he served, he held it in his left hand and hit it between his fingers. Teddy served and returned the ball hard, and he took special delight in making a good placement shot to some corner that his opponent could not reach.

A less strenuous recreation which many Presidents enjoyed was billiards. Washington found delight in the game and played it often. When he was seventeen years old, he paid a visit to a neighboring plantation and offered to show his host what he had recently learned of the art of billiards. The other man, skeptical of Washington's newly acquired skill, suggested that the two play for a small wager. Washington emerged from the table richer by one shilling and threepence, and from that time on he frequently won and lost small bets with his cue. Jefferson also liked the game, and he designed one room at Monticello as a billiard room. But before it could be completed, a law was passed prohibiting public or private billiard tables in Virginia. To some of our straightlaced forefathers billiards was considered a shady pastime conjured up by the devil.

A dreadful uproar occurred when President John Quincy Adams informed Congress that he had purchased for the White House a billiard table, cues, and billiard balls. Although the sum total of this expenditure was only sixty-one dollars, the President's enemies pounced on it as an extravagant waste of funds for articles that were morally degrading. Their attack was so vicious that Adams's friends in Congress had to defend him on the floor of the House against the charge that he was a corruptor of the country's youth. In the end the harassed President paid for the billiard table and equipment out of his own pocket.

When Lincoln was a young lawyer in Illinois, he played billiards frequently but apparently without much skill. "As a constant habit," wrote Carl Sandburg, "he chose as his opponent at billiards a bibulous lawyer of no merit save the negative one of playing billiards as awkwardly and badly as Lincoln himself. It was a strange but not unfamiliar sight to see these two men, who had nothing else in common, playing billiards in an obscure place, sometimes for hours together."

Several other Presidents liked to chalk their cues and aim for the side pocket. Ulysses S. Grant built a billiard room in a part of the old White House conservatory, and he generally would go there for a while after dinner to practice with cue and balls. Puffing large clouds of cigar smoke as he leaned over the table, the President would perfect difficult shots and plot the best strategy for scoring points. Garfield and Benjamin Harrison also were billiard strategists during their leisure hours. When Garfield was a congressman, he played almost every day before dinner, and one of his frequent opponents was a lawyer named Charles H. Reed. Years later, ironically, Reed became the attorney for the man who shot and killed President Garfield.

When Hayes became the Chief Executive, his pious wife banned the serving of liquor at the White House and had the billiard table moved to the basement. Although some of Hayes's successors enjoyed the game, the billiard table did not again occupy a prominent place in the Executive Mansion until the administration of Woodrow Wilson. The second Mrs. Wilson, anxious to find ways to relieve the wartime pressures on her husband, felt that billiards might prove a healthful diversion if the President had a good place to play. So she had a billiard room, complete with a fireplace, fitted out in a section of the ground floor corridor. Her plan produced the desired results, and Wilson not only visited the room for his own amusement, but he also took his daughters there and taught them to play billiards with him.

Wilson also was an ardent bicyclist. Twice he spent the summer bicycling in the British Isles, traveling sometimes thirty miles in a day. When he was a professor at Princeton, he rode a bicycle to class, in tall hat and striped trousers. Tipping his hat to the colleagues he passed, the jaunty professor pedaled along at a steady pace with his coattails blowing in the wind. One day a short distance from Princeton, Wilson came upon a student who was trying out one of those new vehicles called a motorcycle. The student suggested that he tow the professor, and he tossed Wilson a rope that was fastened to the bicycle handlebars. Across the country-side sped the motorcycle, with the bicycle bouncing along behind. But when the two vehicles reached the edge of town, Wilson called to the student to stop. He told the young man that it might not be considered proper for a professor to be seen streaking across the campus behind a motor-driven machine.

Various Presidents, either as youths or adults, in-dulged in other physical pursuits. Washington liked to bowl on the lawn, and Lincoln played a fast, aggressive game of handball. Hayes installed the first croquet court on the White House grounds. Grant was a talented ice skater, and Kennedy played ice hockey and swept down New England slopes on skis. Both the Roosevelts also were fond of winter sports, and as youths they had fun on skates, skis, sleds, and toboggans.

But by far the most popular form of exercise among the White House residents was the simplest of all — walking. To enjoy a brisk, invigorating stroll requires no special skill or physical prowess, no elaborate prepa-rations or cumbersome equipment, and no extended period of time when one must be away from his desk.

Even the most sedentary, unathletic Presidents could find healthful relaxation and recreation in a carefree walk.

James Buchanan and William McKinley were two Chief Executives who relied almost entirely on daily walks to keep themselves fit. Calvin Coolidge disliked most forms of exercise except his mechanical horse, and this would have given his doctors cause for concern had he not strolled along the streets of Washington every morning. Harry Truman was another President whose habit of walking contributed to his stamina and physical well-being. Twirling the gold-headed cane given to him by his Army buddies from the First World War, he set off every morning at seven for a brisk two-mile walk. Truman jogged along at a vigorous pace of 120 steps a minute, with Secret Service men scurrying to keep up. Dr. Wallace H. Graham, his physician remarked, "Mr. Truman was in better condition when he left the White House than when he entered it, and in my opinion, his walking had a lot to do with it."

For a brief time after his inauguration, President Truman was able to stroll down Washington streets undisturbed and almost unnoticed. Before long, however, newspapers began featuring stories about his daily exercise, and soon the famous pedestrian became a sort of Pied Piper, trailed by throngs of reporters, cameramen, and gawking sightseers. The President tried changing his route and time of departure, but he could not escape the crowds that gathered to stare at him. Finally he hit upon a scheme that permitted him to continue his strolls in privacy. He drove in his long, black limousine to various locations in the outskirts of Washington, where he got out and enjoyed his walks in rural seclusion.

Truman's plight as a pedestrian was far different from the undisturbed jaunts that Presidents took in earlier days. William Henry Harrison would leave the White House on foot to do his own marketing. He got up early and trotted out to get chops and steaks for his breakfast. Zachary Taylor liked to stop at markets on his walks and engage the farmers in friendly conversation. Wearing a black broadcloth suit and a silk hat perched on the back of his head, he became a familiar sight on the streets of the capital city. And Abraham Lincoln found satisfaction in rising early and sauntering quietly about the city or visiting a neighboring camp of soldiers before he returned home for breakfast.

Sometimes the Chief Executives would cover an astonishing amount of territory on foot. Both Presidents from the Adams family regularly walked long distances. At the age of eighty-five John Adams's short, stocky legs could still carry him four or five miles over the rocky hills near his Massachusetts home. Jefferson developed the habit of taking long jaunts during his school days, and it was said that in his youth he often walked fourteen miles at a stretch. Benjamin Harrison was another long-distance walker, and he frequently took a ten-mile tramp following his day's work. But among the Presidents the marathon walking champion was undoubtedly Millard Fillmore. In his seventeenth summer he journeyed on foot more than one hundred miles to visit some relatives near Buffalo, and then walked all the way back home.

Strolling was, as one might expect, much too tame for Theodore Roosevelt. He devised "obstacle walks" in which the hikers proceeded from the starting point to the objective in a beeline without making any detours for natural obstacles. In Washington it was considered almost as great an honor to be invited on a Roosevelt "obstacle walk" as it was to play with the Tennis Cabinet. But it was a much more exhausting ordeal than tennis. Up rocky hillsides, down steep ravines, over swift streams (which sometimes could be crossed only by swimming), the President and his walking party struggled. This type of excursion delighted Roosevelt more than did mountain climbing, although he had tried his hand at that sport, too. In fact, he interrupted his honeymoon in Europe to climb the Matterhorn. And he was tramping in the Adirondacks when he learned he had become the youngest President in history.

In 1908 President Roosevelt issued an order that all Marine Corps Company officers be able to march fifty miles in twenty hours, double-timing the last seven hundred yards. Fifty-five years later this same order was dug out of the Corps files and shown to another President, John F. Kennedy. Curious to find out whether the Marines of 1963 were as hardy as those of 1908, President Kennedy suggested to the Corps commandant that his men might be given the same assignment that Roosevelt had concocted.

The modern Marines undertook the marathon hike and came through the experience with flying colors. Moreover, when this achievement was publicized in the newspapers, people throughout the country wanted to copy the Marines and test their own physical fitness. Attempting a fifty-mile hike became a nationwide fad. Boy Scout Tenderfeet hoofed in Illinois, and tenderfooted politicians huffed and puffed in Washington. College fraternity members took to the craze with the same jubilant enthusiasm with which they crowded into telephone booths. At Stanford University students hiked in derbies and sweatshirts; in Seattle they swept over the fifty-mile junket on roller skates.

The President's brother, Robert Kennedy, set out with four Justice Department aides at five o'clock one wintry morning, determined to prove that a member of the First Family could also perform the difficult feat. Striding over icy paths and slushing through mudholes, Kennedy doggedly plodded on. His four aides all tired and dropped out, but the Attorney General finally completed the expedition in under eighteen hours. Even the President and his wife got into the act, but in a much less arduous way. They strolled across the ellipse from Constitution Avenue to the White House, and although Mrs. Kennedy's heels sank into the lawn on the homestretch, they accomplished the task with vigor.

One general observation about our Presidents and their sports should be mentioned in conclusion. Most of the men who became strong and effective Chief Executives were also enthusiastic sportsmen. Whether it was helping to coach football or casting for trout, hunting big game or wrestling in an open square, our greater Presidents generally were active, vigorous participants in the world of sport. Washington, Lincoln, Jefferson, Jackson, Cleveland, Wilson, and both Roosevelts were ardent disciples of one or more facets of outdoor life. And should historians someday decide to place Eisenhower or Kennedy on the list of outstanding Chief Executives, both men would also qualify as sportsmen of the first rank.

Before any future President puts his fishing tackle or golf bags into storage when he moves into the White House, he might ponder what boxer William Mooney said about his sparring partner, Theodore Roosevelt. "A President, like everyone else," observed Mooney, "must play as well as work if he keeps fit, and it was because he managed to get so much out of play that Colonel Roosevelt was able to get so much out of work. And being a good play-fellow, he simply had to be a good man."

IN WRITING this book numerous biographies, diaries, books, magazines, contemporary newspapers, and personal letters were consulted. Certain sources were especially helpful in providing information and specific quotations about the sports of the various Presidents. If you would like to read further, we would suggest some of the following books.

The several volumes by Douglas Southall Freeman entitled *George Washington, A Biography* (Scribner's, 1948–57) are excellent. Another interesting study is *George Washington, The Rebel and the Patriot, 1762–1777* by Rupert Hughes (Morrow, 1926). For more about Jefferson's activities you might read *The Young Jefferson* by Claude Bowers (Houghton Mifflin, 1945). Two outstanding books about Jackson were written by Marquis James: *Andrew Jackson, The Border Captain* (Literary Guild, 1933) and *Andrew Jackson, Portrait of a President* (Bobbs-Merrill, 1937).

Carl Sandburg's works on Lincoln are superbly written. Readers will enjoy both his *Abraham Lincoln, The Prairie Years* (Harcourt, Brace, 1927) and *Abraham Lincoln, The War Years* (Harcourt, Brace, 1939). Lively accounts of Grant's sports can be found in *Captain Sam Grant* by Lloyd Lewis (Little, Brown, 1950).

Grover Cleveland wrote about his outdoor pursuits in *Fishing and Shooting Sketches* (Outing Publishing Company, 1906).

Another helpful work is *Grover Cleveland, A Study in Courage* by Allan Nevins (Dodd, Mead, 1932).

Several books were written by Theodore Roosevelt about his own physical activities. Perhaps a good place to begin reading more about this fascinating President would be his *Autobiography* (Scribner's, 1958). *Theodore Roosevelt's Letters to His Children* (Scribner's, 1926) is also interesting. A handsomely illustrated study is *The Life and Times of Theodore Roosevelt* by Stefan Lorant (Doubleday, 1959).

A helpful book on Taft is *The Life and Times of William Howard Taft* by Henry F. Pringle (Farrar and Rinehart, 1939). Cary Grayson, Wilson's personal physician, tells about the private life of his famous patient in *Woodrow Wilson, An Intimate Memoir* (Holt, 1960). *Woodrow Wilson, Life and Letters* by Ray Stannard Baker relates many interesting experiences.

A book with many entertaining anecdotes about one of our Presidents is *Grace Coolidge and Her Era, The Story of a President's Wife* by Ishbel Ross (Dodd, Mead, 1962). Herbert Hoover describes some of his sports in *The Memoirs of Herbert Hoover, Years of Adventure, 1874–1920* (Macmillan, 1951).

White House Physician by Ross T. McIntire and George Creel (Putnam, 1946) is a helpful book about Franklin D. Roosevelt. So is *Affectionately, F.D.R., A Son's Story of a Lonely Man* by James Roosevelt and Sidney Shalett (Harcourt, Brace, 1959). A good biography of Roosevelt's successor in the White House is *Harry S. Truman* by Alfred Steinberg (Putnam, 1963).

Young Ike by Alden Hatch (Messner, 1953) tells about Eisenhower during the years when he was growing to manhood. *Meet Mr. Eisenhower* by A. Merriman Smith (Harper, 1955) is an excellent account by a White House correspondent. Another helpful book is *Soldier of Democracy, A Biography of Dwight Eisenhower* by Kenneth S. Davis (Doubleday, 1945).

James MacGregor Burns has written a fine biography entitled *John Kennedy, A Political Profile* (Harcourt, Brace, 1959). Another fascinating account is *The Remarkable Kennedys* by Joe McCarthy (Dial Press, 1960).

In addition to the biographies and books written by our Presidents, there are some general sources that provide much interesting information about the sports of our Chief Executives. These include *Annals of American Sport* by John Allen Krout (Yale University Press, 1929); *America Learns to Play* by Foster Rhea Dulles (Appleton-Century, 1940); *Four Centuries of Sport in America, 1490–1890* by Herbert Manchester (The Derrydale Press, 1931); *American Sports (1785–1835)* by Jennie Holliman (The Seeman Press, 1931); *Starling of the White House* by Thomas Sugrue (Simon and Schuster, 1946); *The Health of the Presidents* by Rudolph Marx (Putnam, 1960); and *Forty-two Years in the White House* by Irwin Hood Hoover (Houghton Mifflin, 1934).